SHADY LADY

Also by Ruth Gordon

Books:

RUTH GORDON: *An Open Book*

MYSELF AMONG OTHERS

MY SIDE: *The Autobiography of Ruth Gordon*

OVER TWENTY-ONE

YEARS AGO

THE LEADING LADY

A VERY RICH WOMAN

Films:

ADAM'S RIB (with Garson Kanin)

PAT AND MIKE (with Garson Kanin)

THE MARRYING KIND (with Garson Kanin)

A DOUBLE LIFE (with Garson Kanin)

THE ACTRESS

SHADY LADY

A NOVEL BY

Ruth Gordon

ARBOR HOUSE   *New York*

SHADY LADY

1

A HOT July day.

Ninety-sixth Street and Broadway.

A hot July day could be good at the beach, Far Rockaway? Who had the big house there? Ray Comstock, owner of the Princess Theatre. Was he a pansy? He never tried to get into a girl's pants.

Far Rockaway would have to be cooler. Or somewhere there was an electric fan. Here in a small apartment, second floor front, the heat came up from the hot Broadway sidewalk. Maybe a sip of Old Grandad? Have it and wonder how she, Winona Lloyd, the great redhead that used to be in the Ziegfeld Follies, got to sleeping with Eddie Schmidt in his sweaty two rooms? Have the Old Grandad, a hot July day needs *something*. She poured and took a sip. Being laid by Eddie Schmidt was a long way from being laid by Larry Dineen under a Winona, Minnesota bush. That was the first time, then Rex in Chicago, then Dennis at the Sherman House in Chicago and in New York at the Algonquin, Mortimer at the Hotel Claridge. The Sherman House and Algonquin and the Claridge would have electric fans. Today was hotter than hot Glorieta out in New Mexico where she was born, but she'd still pick New York and Ninety-sixth. Glorieta, nothing ever happened, here at least something went on.

Another sip. The Ansonia tower suite where Ziegfeld kept her was probably a breeze. Julius had fans in his private car. He was no good doing it, but right up there with the stocks and emeralds. How did she get those guys? Learned how in the back office of Mr. Holbrook's hardware store on Station Street in Winona? What a route! From a hardware store to Chicago, New York, Palm Beach, Paris, to a walk-up, Broadway and West Ninety-sixth!

The doorbell rang.

She reached for a lacy wrapper that had seen a lot of better days. "Come in."

The door was opened by a dowdy-looking middle-aged woman. "I'm *The Daily Mirror* about a interview for our 'Where Are the Former Ziegfeld Girls, July, 1930?' "

"That's me. Throw his pants off that chair. Want a beer? Old Grandad?"

"Uh, no thanks. Would you prefer I call you Miss Lloyd or Mrs. Eddie Schmidt?"

Winona laughed. "The janitor calls me Mrs. to make the place look more respectable, but for *The Mirror* say Winona Lloyd."

"I'm Rachel Lowery."

Winona laughed again. "I knew a girl in Minnesota called Rachel. I bet nobody's banged her *yet.*"

Even an interviewer from *The Daily Mirror* got a hoist. "In—in Minnesota was this friend?"

"Who said she was a friend? But you're right on Minnesota. I went there when I was five. My God, twenty-six crazy years ago! A sexy old man thought I was six, but he didn't feel me up, another one did. He was the first. Did y'like *your* first?"

"You a—you a—Mr. Ziegfeld said you were the most beautiful girl in his Follies."

Winona nodded. "And I was."

"The—uh—the swing? I remember you swinging out over the heads of the audience having supper at tables."

"It looked like the customers were getting a look, but they made me wear tights. Of course, I had long hair then. So did Peggy Hopkins and Helen Lee Worthing, but Carmelita Geraghty got hers cut off. Ziggy got Irene Castle's man that cut *hers* to cut mine. It looked great short. Ziggy was wild about it. Know what else? Me having three freckles on my bottom, one the right, two the left. They'd send Flo into labor. His wife Billie Burke had red hair too, but I guess no three freckles."

"Uh-huh."

"Y'wonder how I'm Ninety-sixth and Broadway, a walk-up, living with Ziegfeld's bookkeeper that's a certified accountant and likes to think of when the closest he could get to me was put my salary in a envelope every week?"

"Uh—Miss Lloyd, you—you have a lot to tell. You certainly lived a lot of life in your thirty-one years. How *did* you come from the Ziegfeld roof to be Mrs . . . " She referred to her notes. "To Mrs. Eddie Schmidt?"

"Anyone ever tell you Ziegfeld was a great lay? He had me in the eighth floor tower suite down Broadway at the Hotel Ansonia. I bet they got a electric fan there. He and his wife were in the tower suite below and y'don't think I didn't cheat on him, do you? Like he cheated on his wife Billie Burke, then started cheatin' on me. But I could get anyone, I was a beauty and could do it great. Who says no to that? The richest man in the state of California set me up in the damnedest apartment on Nob Hill in San Francisco."

"Why did you break up with Mr. Ziegfeld?"

"Oh, Jack Bedford, remember him? He got me on the stuff. He was good in bed or in a car or under the table, but he got me on the stuff. Why '*but*'? I liked it. Anybody did that had go."

"And—"

"After Jack, I was looked after by Julius Schwab, the art collector. He loved *my* art and the rest of me. Then Archie, the California guy I was telling about. My *start* was an old man, then a high-school kid that boasted he had four girls in freshman class and the English teacher. With my looks and somebody showing me how, I knew I'd make it and I knew that's what I had talent for so I left for Chicago to go to the Chicago Musical College, run by Flo Ziegfeld's father. Imagine! Cheated with an actor engaged to my mother's best friend, Eva Dill—you maybe heard of her? Then I quit her guy and married the star, Dennis Ryan. He was great, but I cheated with a rich old guy, big corporation lawyer, Mortimer Burrage, who got me in the Princess Theatre musical show. A power guy except in bed. He set me up at Broadway and Forty-fourth, the Hotel Claridge. Some different to Broadway and Ninety-sixth! Dennis was a sweetie and gave me a divorce. Nights I wasn't at the Claridge, I was at the mansion Morty owned at Tarrytown up the Hudson. Every place had fans."

"*Well,* Miss Lloyd," said the lady reporter, "if you had it to do—uh—over, would you do anything different?"

Winona nodded. "I never should've cut my hair."

"Well—thanks." Miss Lowery gathered up her things,

dropped them, picked them up and stumbled out of the room.

Winona poured herself another shot, took her wrapper off, stretched out on the bed. How long since anybody'd wanted to do a piece on her? Now *The Daily Mirror* sent that pixie all the way up to Ninety-sixth Street. And why was she still here? She'd thought she'd stay with Eddie till something went right, but that was last October. Last October to hot July? She counted on her fingers nine months, like they counted if they were looking for a baby. Did she wish she'd had a baby? No more than she wished she'd sleep tonight with Eddie Schmidt. The start of last October everything great, today Ziegfeld's bookkeeper. Why had she lost out? She'd handled herself fine since she was five years old in Glorieta, New Mexico, and saw Mr. Barney feeling up Nita Macchi in the woods, and he kissed her and said to come see him in his Glorieta Garage and Implement store.

What was that? Twenty-six years ago? A lifetime . . .

2

"It's no more than a ten-minute walk from Glorieta," Mrs. Brigham told the Wells Fargo Express man, "but with my heavy Gladstone bag . . . When you come down from Santa Fe Thursday, you go right by where a lady's going to have a baby. Let me ride with you."

She didn't deliver a baby unless she liked the people. She'd come out west when her husband Charlie died to look after her brother. Two years later he was no more and had made her the heir to his land and money. She wasn't rich but in no need.

Dr. Graham was. "I need you," he'd said. "I've got to get my mother back from Pocatello. Could you help Mrs. Beryl Lloyd? She's a young widow. Sad story. She's due on the fourteenth."

On the twelfth, Wells Fargo's two black horses pulled up and Mrs. Brigham got down. "Stop off in a couple of weeks," she told the driver.

He wrote it on a slip of paper, stuck it in his cap. The horses shook off the red dust, whinnied, and were on their way.

Even for June, the heat was awful. Pretty Mrs. Lloyd

poured two glasses of root beer. An old white dog lay in the room. "This is Chalky."

"Hello, Chalky."

"At home we had lemonade when we had company, but out here, no one ever saw a lemon." She smiled at Mrs. Brigham and looked even prettier. Her red hair in the sunlight turned to gold.

Mrs. Brigham smiled back at her. "You got pretty hair. Where was home?"

"Weymouth, Massachusetts. Ever hear of it?"

Mrs. Brigham nodded. "That's as far east as you can get. Your people still live there?"

Mrs. Lloyd shook her head. "My father didn't want to live there after mama. He'd had enough north wind to last him, so with the insurance money and the factory pension, he took off on a freighter for California. From Santa Rosa out there, he wrote it was some cold and got on a boat to Honolulu."

"Why, that's where I got a pineapple from. A man knew Charlie—he was my husband—and after Charlie died, he sent it all the way to Glorieta."

" 'It's always mild,' said papa." She smiled. It was nice to have someone to talk to.

"What's your father's name?"

"White. Papa's father named him Ulysses after General Grant. Everybody else's father was Herbert or Alfred or Donald. Hey, will you be able to manage? There's only one bedroom." Her face clouded over. "Jack was planning—" She didn't go on.

Mrs. Brigham reached for her hand. "All I need is something to lie down on somewhere. Minnesota's

13

where I come from. Minnesota is my home. Winona, Minnesota. I guess it's the best place ever was."

"I was in a show playing one-nighters and we were headed for towns in Minnesota, but I got married before that, so then no more shows."

"If you weren't due I'd ask Wells Fargo to stop by and give us a hitch there, you'd like Winona!"

3

EVEN THE SHADY spots were suffocating. Across the road, Mrs. Macchi's corn patch had turned dry yellow, a big hot sunflower dragged its head. Mrs. Macchi, short and fat, fanned herself with a cottonwood branch. Nothing was moving on the long road, one end of which stretched back to Glorieta, the other disappeared in the sun. Her seven-year-old daughter raced past her out of the house. "Where you *go?*"

Nita pointed somewhere and raced toward it.

"You crazy." Adjusting her wrapper, Mrs. Macchi ambled across the road. "Hot," she said to the old white dog lying inside the gate. He rolled up one eyelid, then dropped it. Mrs. Macchi looked in the door. Mrs. Brigham was hemming some diapers.

"How is?"

From the bedroom came a moan.

"Pretty soon now."

"Too goddamn hot have baby." Mrs. Macchi lowered her fat self into a rush-bottomed chair that quivered and sighed. She put her hands on her knees and peered through the bedroom door. "Hot day."

The white face on the pillow didn't answer.

"She too white. I bring wine."

Mrs. Brigham shook her head. "Wine's no good. What a climate! I wish I'd never left the East."

"No hot?"

A scream from the bedroom. Then a scream and a groan. Mrs. Macchi struggled up, rolled toward the door. "You like fan?" She offered the cottonwood.

Beads of sweat stood out on the white face. "Mrs. Brigham?" It was a weak whisper.

"Mrs. Brig, you *come!*" Mrs. Macchi's voice wasn't weak. It rumbled like winter thunder.

Mrs. Brigham put her apron to the sweat beads. "You're fine. Just relax, then push hard like you'd push a snow shovel down your front walk in Weymouth."

The old dog rested his chin on the sheet, anxiety on his white fur face. "Chalky." A hand crept out and held Chalky's head.

"Push, then rest, then push." Mrs. Brigham went back to the chair by the window, threaded a needle.

Mrs. Macchi sank down on the end of the sofa. "No husband," she crossed herself. "He lovely man, no good for this country. Too pretty."

"Give me the East. Roses all over the fences and

climbing up the side of your house like the town's covered with wallpaper. Green trees, not these runts, here the shade is hot as the sun."

A groan.

"In Winona maple trees and oak line Prospect Avenue, and lilacs every yard. Charlie and I lived in Number Sixteen Prospect Avenue, Winona, Minnesota. You don't know where that is, but I like to say the address."

"Pretty house?"

Mrs. Brigham glanced out the window. "If you happen to like a white house with green blinds, a gravel walk, not dirty red sand."

A stabbing cry.

"I'm starting the hot water." Mrs. Brigham put aside her sewing. "My kitchen was white with set tubs, no dust." She blew some off a kettle and shoved it over the hot coals. "Every kettle I had was white."

A cry.

She shoved a smaller kettle on and saw that towels were handy, got two strips of strong white cotton and tied one to the end of the bed. "When the pain comes, pull hard," she said to the face on the pillow. "Mrs. Macchi, tie this other strip. My parlor had a cherrywood armchair, cherry center table, and a silk rep sofa." She leaned closer to the pillow. "Pull, Mrs. Lloyd." She went back in the kitchen. "And a green shade on the gasolier the color of my spring lettuce."

Mrs. Macchi closed the white hand around the strip. "You pull, darlin'."

Suddenly the hands pulled convulsively.

"Nice necklace?" In the window was the head and shoulders of a fat old Indian.

"Come to door. Lady goddamn sick."

Mrs. Macchi went out on the steps. "You new people?"

The old Indian shook his head. "Walking by."

"Where from?"

"From Colorado." He held up a turquoise-mounted brass pin. "For gentleman's necktie?"

"No gentleman. You got for baby?"

"Nice turquoise ring?"

A long groan.

The fat old traveler pointed to the front step. "I sit down. You take plenty time."

4

BERYL SAT UNDER the cottonwood tree, her first time out. In the crib near the door the baby slept. Chalky tried to keep his eyes on Beryl, but he fell asleep.

"Know what gives me the pip?" Mrs. Brigham pointed past Mrs. Macchi's corn patch to a sign. "Barney's Garage and Implement Co. Why's he have to say 'Implement'? Can't he say 'tools' like everybody else?"

Beryl laughed. "You're a sketch. 'Implement—' "

"Yoo-hoo." Coming across the road was Mrs. Macchi. Chalky growled, reared up, then collapsed.

"Chicky soup." Mrs. Macchi held out a brown pottery bowl. "Goes down, sits there."

Beryl patted the fat brown arm. "You're just a sweetheart."

"Hot sweetheart." She broke off a branch from overhead and heaved herself into a chair. "My mama have red silk fan so she get cool, like ice in water they drink down to Albuquerk."

"Wish I had some." Beryl closed her eyes to remember.

"Albuquerk they got ice from last winter goddamn cold."

"Oh, they keep ice all summer in Winona," Mrs. Brigham said. "Chip off a piece, drop it in a glass of lemonade. When Eaton's Pond freezes deep, Mr. Swenson hauls it to his big shed."

Mrs. Macchi stopped fanning. "Shed?"

"Icehouse. Swenson's Icehouse. They pack it under straw and old newspapers. I'd put a Swenson's yellow card in the window, turn the number on the card to twenty-five—fifteen if I don't want much—thirty-five to make a freezer of ice cream. Ever eat raspberry ice cream, Beryl? We had it Sundays from berries off our bushes right out back." She turned to Mrs. Macchi. "Ever hear of a raspberry?"

Mrs. Macchi shook her head.

Beryl laughed. "Where I lived, a Swede ran a bakeshop and made doughnuts with raspberry jam in the middle. No hole, raspberry jam." She laughed again.

"Laugh some more." Mrs. Macchi gave her a thump on the shoulders. "Goddamn."

"In Winona, kids with a lard pail go around selling a quart for a dime."

Mrs. Macchi stopped fanning. "What color?"

"Red."

Mrs. Macchi fanned harder. "I like see snow, you have some?"

Beryl looked past the dust and the heat. "Winters every windowsill looks like somebody lay down a white sleeve, high drifts cover the rhododendrons. There're big bushes in the front yard. Down the street come sleigh bells. A sleigh is a carriage built to go over the snow."

Mrs. Brigham nodded agreement. "Oh, winters! Early September Charlie laid in a ton of coal from Soren's coalyard by the Burlington tracks and hired Albert Sundberg to cut logs for our fireplace. Beryl, did you go to bed with a hot brick?"

"An old whiskey bottle of papa's with hot water." She turned to Mrs. Macchi. "Papa moved away when mama died."

Mrs. Macchi crossed herself.

Beryl looked past the dusty junipers and jackpines. "I'm kind of stranded. Jack was such a grand fellow—"

Mrs. Macchi reached out and gave her another thump. "Now you got a grand, goddamn baby, we get drunk, I get wine."

5

Mrs. BRIGHAM snapped the thread off the diaper she'd hemmed. "I better watch for Wells Fargo. You had any more thoughts about anything? Mr. Lloyd have any people?"

Beryl looked around the room as though she'd never seen it. "Boston, Commonwealth Avenue. He graduated from Massachusetts Tech and went as mining engineer with the Calumet and Hecla Copper people in Michigan. The both of us from Massachusetts and we go to Michigan to meet. Hancock was a one-night stand the show I was in played. And seven weeks to that day, Jack got off the train in Green Bay, Wisconsin, and the Justice of the Peace married us after the matinee. Jack and me and a girl in the show, Eva Dill, stood in his parlor and the Justice of the Peace's wife. Jack had invited his folks, but they wrote if you want to marry somebody cheap, they didn't want any more to do with him. Only when it didn't look—well, you know, not encouraging, I wrote . . . Hey, don't go back yet."

"Sure not. But maybe next week you'll be sick of me."

6

"HI," SAID Mrs. Macchi to the baby sleeping in the crib, then padded out to the kitchen. Beryl was in the backyard, working at the big tub. Mrs. Brigham, clothespin in her mouth, was hanging up a petticoat.

"You goddamn wear too much. Joe bring letter."

"Thanks." Beryl looked at it, then at Mrs. Brigham. The color had gone out of her face. She looked hard at the white envelope. "It's from Boston."

"Maybe look in?" suggested Mrs. Macchi. "Then you know some more."

"It's from Jack's family lawyer. I don't want to hear it by myself."

HATHAWAY & PAGE
91 DEVONSHIRE PLACE
BOSTON, MASS.

July 21, 1898

Mrs. Beryl Lloyd
General Delivery
Glorieta, N.M.
Dear Madam:
Our client, Mr. J. Minot Lloyd, wishes to be

informed if his son, the late John Minot Lloyd, Jr., left an heir. Should this be the case, our client wishes it known that he would be willing to adopt the infant legally to be raised hereafter by him with the provision that the mother make no effort henceforth to see or claim the infant. My client would, of course, make a mutually satisfactory financial settlement on said infant's mother—

Beryl couldn't go on.

Mrs. Macchi used her loud voice, "Goddamn fresh letter. Throw away."

Mrs. Brigham looked into the distance. "Shouldn't we hail Wells Fargo? What's here?"

"Jack."

"Thoughts of him will come along. In Winona your thoughts will be, like Mrs. Macchi says, 'more goddam comfortable.' "

Mrs. Macchi nodded. "You say it good."

"I'm glad I didn't drop dead. I never said that word." She listened to a gurgle from the bedroom. "Know who I'd like to parade in a go-cart under our maples on Prospect? Her. A maple on Brook Street is higher than Dr. Jensen's house, even counting the lightning rods. April, it gets red buds that look like buttons on a church pew cushion. A gale off the river lands them on the sidewalk. When it rains, it makes the air sweet."

Another gurgle. Beryl went in and picked up the baby. "They smell like leftover Christmas candy."

The little head had curls of red hair, redder then Beryl's. "Winona sounds like where things go fine." She looked down at the small red head. "Winona. It's going to be her name."

Mrs. Brigham flushed. "You don't mean it!"

"Winona Lloyd. Jack loved things to be pretty."

"His baby's pretty. Now she has a pretty name."

Mrs. Macchi nodded. "I *like* a place has ice."

7

YESTERDAY HAD BEEN Winona's fifth birthday.

She pushed through the scratchy junipers toward the sound of the brook. Had she come a long way from where she lived? That was allowed, now she was five years old. Would the brook lead her home? Her handful of limp wildflowers she put down on the bank and, pulling off her dusty moccasins, let the cool brown water curl around her feet. When the sky was pink behind the Glorieta Chain, didn't that mean it would get dark?

"Yoo-hoo!" she called. "Yoo-hoo!" Then cupped her hands, drank some water, cold as the Albuquerque water Mrs. Macchi talked about, then gave the flowers a bath. Their stems hung down like worms, a few came loose and spun away. She'd pick some more on the way back. And where was the way back? The sky had gotten pinker, like the inside of a Rocky Ford melon. "Yoo-hoo!" Somebody had to come and look for her and wouldn't they come down to the brook for a drink? She made a bed of scraggly cottonwood leaves, laid out the flowers and covered them with more leaves. Past the jackpine she heard a laugh. Somebody in a red cotton dress was over there with somebody. The somebody in the red cotton dress was lying on a man's lap and laughing. It was little Nita Macchi and Mr. Barney was tickling her under her red skirt.

"Yoo-hoo!" called Winona.

Mr. Barney jumped. So did Nita Macchi.

"Go *away!*" yelled Nita.

Nobody had ever told her to go away.

Mr. Barney came down to the brook and took her hand. "We're planning a surprise," he said kindly. "And if you tell your mother or Nita's mother, you'll spoil it. Have a pink candy?" He held out some shiny pink taffy in fluted silver paper. Nita made a face at her and went in back of some bushes. "You're a sweet little girl." Mr. Barney lifted her up in his arms, cuddled her close to him. "Don't tell me how old you are, let me guess. I bet you're six."

She shook her head. "I'm five. My birthday was yesterday."

"Here's a birthday kiss." His mouth tasted like cigar smoke, but he kissed her sweetly. "Come in my store, I'll have a present for you. I wouldn't want anybody to tell our secret."

"I wouldn't."

"Here's a birthday kiss to grow on." He put her down. "Come along, Nita." He held Winona's hand and they walked to the dirt road, where tied to a scrub oak was a horse and buggy. "Go along," he said and gave her a little pat. Then he kissed Nita Macchi *hard,* not sweetly.

"Did that hurt?" asked Winona admiringly.

Nita Macchi glared at her.

"Walk fast, and I'll watch you go," said Mr. Barney.

Winona drew back. "She's mean and I don't want to."

He took Nita by the shoulders and shook her. "You be nice or I'll take your drawers off and spank your fat bottom until it's red." He kissed her hard again, jumped into his buggy, hit the horse with his whip and rattled out of sight toward Glorieta.

"You tell and I'll come over in the night and *kill* you!" Nita shoved her so suddenly Winona fell in the dust. She got up and looked defiant.

"My mother wouldn't *let* you kill me." She crossed to the other side of the road.

"I'll put a rattlesnake in your bed that'll suck all the blood out of you."

"I don't like you, but I never tell a secret." She walked faster.

8

WINONA BRUSHED her teeth, then looked at the yellow chickens painted on her toothbrush that Mrs. Brigham's friend had painted for her. "Can we start my new book Grandpa White sent me for my birthday?" She put her shapeless black pussycat in bed with its head on the pillow and lay down beside it.

"Lost Dottie," read Beryl.

Winona sat bolt upright. "What's *that?"*

"The name of it."

"What's it about?" She asked apprehensively.

"About a little girl, I guess—'One evening—' "

"Mama, read another one."

"Don't you want to find out if I'm right?—'One evening when papa came home, mama met him with a frightened look. She said that little Dottie was lost. Her brother Rob had called until he was hoarse.' "

"What did he call?"

"Yoo-hoo, I guess."

"I don't like it, mama."

" 'It was nearly dark, so Dottie's papa got a lantern, took Ranger the dog, and Rob, for though he was a small boy, he had bright eyes. Where was little Dottie?' "

"Mama, read another one." She burst into tears and pulled the sheet over her head.

"Baby, it's only a story."

Winona sobbed, "Mama, I don't want a secret."

"We won't have any." Beryl had never seen her cry so.

"She's going to kill me. She and Mr. Barney have a surprise, and he's nice but she's mean. Mama, I was lost and then I saw Nita Macchi and Mr. Barney that has that sign Mrs. Brigham hates and Nita Macchi got mad because I spoiled the surprise they had. But Mr. Barney gave me a good pink candy and thought I was six years old. He said I'm very big for five going on six, but Nita Macchi made a face at me before she put her drawers on and Mr. Barney kissed me and said if she was mean he'd spank her. But he rode away and she shook me. It's a secret, mama, and I said I wouldn't tell."

Beryl held her tight. "Could you stop crying if I tell you mine?"

"If it's a secret, you *can't!*" she sobbed.

"We'll swap."

"What?" Her head was pressed tight to Beryl's neck.

"Chalky and you and I are going somewheres."

"Where?" She still didn't raise her head.

"I'll give you three guesses and one hint. Here's the hint. Where the houses are white and they have lilac bushes and—"

"To Winona?" Her face was still buried.

"Tomorrow we'll walk into Glorieta and swap our secret with Mrs. Brigham and ask if she'll come with us. But you and I and Chalky will go anyway."

Winona cautiously lifted her head. "It only took me *one hint,* mama."

9

THE TRAIN WHISTLED, the green fields went slower, the Winona Tool and Gear Company slid by.

"Along here somewhere is Swenson's Ice Company. There's Butler's Pond, Winona! They skate there in winter."

"Like Hans Brinker."

"Who?"

"Like *Hans Brinker and the Silver Skates* Grandpa White sent me."

The rain slapped against the train window and over the wet trees, but Mrs. Brigham saw fine weather and the town she loved.

"Winona!" the conductor shouted.

"Here I am!" She stepped out into the aisle. The conductor helped lift their things onto the station platform, then shouted, "All aboard!" and was the only one to get on.

"Delicious smell!" Mrs. Brigham took a deep breath.

Winona stared around her. "They got it dirty."

Mrs. Brigham wasn't troubled. "Any place is dirty near the railroad tracks. It's not dirty as a cactus."

A smile flickered on Winona's face. "My favorite color is red velvet."

"This rain won't hurt us, it's just a summer rain to make the flowers grow," said Mrs. Brigham. "This street we turn down is Station Street."

Winona stared up and down the street. "Where's the maples?"

"Around on Brook. Here's Mr. Hardy's jewelry store, Mrs. Grant's Dry Goods."

Winona looked anxious. "Are the lilacs on Brook?"

Mrs. Brigham looked as though she could smell them. "Next May you'll be dizzy."

They turned a corner.

"Why lookit!" Mrs. Brigham exclaimed. "George Snowden got his own store. George used to deliver groceries for Mr. Backus and now it says 'George Snowden's Elite Market' on his awning."

A nice-looking young man stepped out. White apron, sleeves rolled up.

"George, I'm back." She and Beryl stood under the awning. "And I brought these good people with me. Beryl, this is George Snowden. George, this is Beryl Lloyd. And this is—"

"I'm the one they named this place for. I'm Winona."

"Is that a fact?"

"It's the other way around," said Beryl. "I can't make her see the difference."

Mrs. Brigham put her hand on George's arm. "George, search the world, there's no spot to equal this one."

"Is that a fact?"

"We're going to be at Mrs. Helmersen's Boarding House until we get us a home of our own."

"Wait." He went into the store.

"Isn't he lovely? They're all like that."

"For the young lady."

"Mama, it's a glass horse!"

Beryl nodded. "It's to eat. Say thank you."

"Thank you. I never eat glass."

Beryl laughed. "It's barley sugar. I knew things would be great here."

They turned onto Fayette Street. "Which one is it, Mrs. Brigham?" Winona hopped up and down.

"The light brown with—"

"You said all the houses were white."

"How do, Mrs. Brigham," called Mrs. Helmersen from the front door.

"How do, Mrs. Helmersen. This is Beryl Lloyd I brought and this is Winona."

"Some people think I'm named for the town and some people think the town's named for me."

"My goodness! How old are you, dear?"

"Five, but a man thought I was six." Her face clouded over. Beryl gave her hand a squeeze.

"Lay your coats down, I'll dry 'em off."

The hall had a door to the office and a door to the parlor. Back of the parlor through double doors was the dining room, table set for twelve. The house smelled like soup.

"Your room looks on the garden." Mrs. Helmersen led them upstairs to a brown room with a brown bed and a cot.

"Fine," said Beryl.

"Fine," Mrs. Brigham agreed.

Winona nodded. "Fine for our dog, too, when he gets here. He'll be worn out, but I'll keep him in bed a day."

10

Florence Swenson would like
the pleasure of your company
at her sixth birthday party
at 2:30 on July 19th, 1903, at
16 Fayette Street.

"Mama, I only played with her one time and she wants me to come to her party." Winona's face turned pink. "Mama, she wrote me the first letter I ever got. I'll go say I'll come."

Beryl looked out at the rain. "Want to print a letter to her? It's more grown-up. You can use my good stationery. Get a pencil."

"Mama, not a *pencil!*"

"Well, what if we spill ink on Mrs. Helmersen's floor?"

"My red crayon?"

"All right."

Winona stood in front of the bureau. "Dear Florence, is how it begins, isn't it? I know how to print *D.* What's after?"

Mrs. Brigham came in.

"Want to watch me write my first letter? What comes after *D,* mama? Mama, help me, what comes after *D?*"

11

"Number forty-one!" Mr. Waldemar, the real estate agent stopped in front of a light-green clapboard two-family house that could use some paint.

Winona gave it a quick look. "It's no good."

"You haven't even seen it." Beryl followed Mrs. Brigham up the walk.

"Houses would be white, you said, this one's vomit color."

"Imaginative." Mr. Waldemar's tone was admiring.

"Would they paint it white?" asked Mrs. Brigham.

"They might. Troop up the path. Ever see a bigger key?" He chose a big iron one from his ring. "There's nice people have the ground floor, Mr. and Mrs. Chapman, no children."

"Every house had lilacs, mama."

"You and I'll set out the bushes. Two purple, two white."

Winona rushed to her. "Hug me, mama. Did you ever say I told a secret?"

"You *didn't,* we swapped."

"Notice the stairs?" Mr. Waldemar swung open the front door. "They're wider than most. Your hall floor is made of larch. Larch is a tree very admired for a polished floor. Very unusual, maybe because the wood comes high. Here's your parlor. Two windows. Lets you see all Sanburn Street and the side one looks out on your neighbor, Neff. German extraction. They have two boys, good ones."

"Does the fireplace draw?" asked Mrs. Brigham.

He struck a big wooden match and held it in the chimney. It flared straight up. And the parlor smelled like sulphur.

"Notice this buff brick mantle. My wife and I think highly of brick. Here's your dining room."

"Mama, I'm hungry."

Mr. Waldemar reached into his pocket and brought out a nickel, a brass key, a lemon drop with a flake of tobacco clinging to it. "Have it," he said.

"What do you say, Winona?"

"It's dirty!"

"So it is." Mr. Waldemar noticed the flake of tobacco.

"Paint and wallpaper can do a lot, Beryl, what do you think?"

Mr. Waldemar went through the kitchen and opened a door. "This upstairs porch looks down on two apple trees, the three gnarled ones are cherry. Beyond that tall grass the land finishes with a steep drop and a stone wall to mark the Winona Grammar School playgrounds."

Beryl and Mrs. Brigham nodded to each other. "Draw up the lease," Mrs. Brigham told him. "Beryl, want to go to Minneapolis tomorrow? When the paint's dry we can move in our things."

Winona leaped up into the air. "I choose a brass bed, mama, with knobs on it."

Beryl caught her excitement. "What time's the train?"

"The 6:00 A.M. has us to Minnie by seven-thirty. Stores open at—"

"And pink rosebud wallpaper for our parlor and baby green like Florence—"

"You can't say baby green, only baby blue."

"Baby green with a piano like Florence's. And some pincushion candy like at her birthday. When's *my* birthday? Oh, I had it."

"But next June fourteenth you'll be in first grade," reminded Mrs. Brigham. "You can bring children home from school. Twelve makes a dandy birthday party. We'll have pink cake, pink candles in pink plaster rosebuds and I'll make us a freezer of strawberry ice cream. June's early for raspberries."

"Florence goes to second grade, but I'll ask her," Winona bowed her head. "Dear God, I love everybody and this floor. What's its name, Mr. Waldemar?"

"Imaginative. Its name is larch."

She knelt down and kissed it. "Dear God, thank you for our larch floor. I *love* larch. Amen."

12

"Isn't this a dandy kettle?" Mrs. Brigham, head wrapped in a towel, was hammering open a crate of supplies they'd bought in Minneapolis. "We'll have dandy soup and pot roast out of this, and just right to can tomatoes when a huckster comes along."

"What's a huckster?" asked Winona.

"Man in a wagon sells vegetables."

"George Snowden's *my* best huckster."

"Oh, George isn't a huckster. George has his own store."

"I like him anyway."

Beryl came in dragging a big bundle. "Who'll help me lay this rug?"

"I have to see my best friend," said Winona.

"Who is it *this* week?"

"George Snowden. I may marry him."

"That's silly."

"Don't you want me to get married?"

"In time."

"Well, don't I have to think first?"

Outside there was a clatter. It was Roney's big red wagon, drawn by two stocky horses. Winona dashed down the stairs.

"Your name Brigham, little girl?" asked the driver.

"Heaven forbid! She's our friend helped us escape from Glorieta in New Mexico. Pleased to meet you. Some people say 'How do?' What do *you* say?"

Mr. Roney looked surprised. "Say, what *do* I?"

His boy, Buster, rolled down from the back of the wagon and all at once the house was awhirl. Mr. Roney and Buster carried up the dining room table. Good thing the stairs were wide as Mr. Waldemar had pointed out. Beryl and Mrs. Brigham shuttled up and down with chairs. The parlor sofa spread out wider and wider, then all at once went up. Mrs. Brigham's bed got up and Beryl's and Winona's and the sewing table, but a bureau wouldn't go around the curve at the top, then it went around and the other bureau, the same size, went easily.

"Hi!" someone called. "Something here for Miss Winona Lloyd." George Snowden was lifting a big something out of his grocery wagon.

Winona shouted out the window. "George, I was coming to see you!" Her head disappeared.

Mrs. Brigham looked out. "Hello, George. What you got there?"

"Just something."

Winona tore past Beryl on the stairs and raced down the front walk. "I bet you anything it's a doll's house." She tore at the brown paper. Beryl came down the walk.

"You folks aren't the only ones who can put a house together."

Why did Beryl's face turn pink?

"Mama, it's got a stove with real stove lids and a

36

handle to lift them off. Mama, I love George next to you and God."

"Do I see lace curtains?" asked Mrs. Brigham.

"Emma McFarland made them and the bed pillows and comforters."

Mr. Roney looked. "You didn't need stuff from Minnie, you could live in *that.*"

Chalky strolled into the group.

"Dog, you look wore out," said Mr. Roney.

"It's living in a boarding house. He detests it. That's my new word, George."

"Buster, would you detest a little rest on the ride home? Hop in the back." He turned to the others. "You get awful tired when you're fifteen."

13

"It's my first day of school, mama, they kill you if you come late."

She held tight to Beryl's hand as they walked up Sanburn to Wabasha, around the corner and down the hill. "I'm not going to look, mama, till I get there. When's my birthday, mama? I forgot."

"June fourteenth. Yoo-hoo, Mrs. Emery!"

Louise Emery and Winona clutched each other, then

held hands as they went in. First-grade teacher, Miss Thatcher, was old with curly white hair, "What's your name?"

"Winona Lloyd."

"You people just moved into the Chapmans' house." She wrote something and looked at Louise.

"Louise Emery."

"Your papa has a tool shop down to the river. Sit down, girls."

Winona pulled Louise to the back of the room. "She's a witch, let's hate her."

Miss Thatcher rapped her desk. "I'm going to give you busy work until I get things straightened out. In your desks are small cards with a letter on them. Spell five words correctly and you will get a gold star when I come round."

Winona shivered. C-A-T. One word. She had to win. D-O-G. Two. C-O-W. Three. She *had* to get a gold star. Winona! W-I-N-O-N-A. Four. One more.

"One more minute, children."

F lay next to *L*. What did F-L spell? She pushed an *E* and an *M* together. F-L-E-M. "I got a gold star," she whispered to Louise. "She's not a witch. I love her. For my birthday party next June I'm going to invite you and ten children and Florence Swenson. You'll get it written in a letter, then *you* have to write me a letter to say yes."

14

BERYL TOOK Winona's white feather-stitched challis party dress out of the closet. "Wear your Dresden sash."

"Why do they call it Dresden?"

They were going to spend Sunday at Captain Humphrey's. He had been captain of the *Columbia,* the ship Beryl's father had made two voyages in. One voyage, they had shipped out of Boston and gone round Cape Horn to Callao with Mrs. Humphrey and little Mabel and young Fred Humphrey along. Now, from Honolulu, Ulysses White wrote that the Captain and Mrs. Humphrey and Mabel had come west to be near Fred and his family upriver at Wabasha. "Go see them and pay my regards."

"When did you see them last?" asked Mrs. Brigham.

"Oh, years ago. Mama and papa and I went on a trolley and once they drove over from Hingham. Papa was so pleased they were coming, he and I walked up the hill to Peterson's, the florist, and bought a dozen red tulips."

Today wasn't the time of year for tulips so Beryl and Winona walked over to Mr. Luard's on Pine Street and bought a dozen red carnations with asparagus fern.

39

The Captain and Mrs. met them at the C.M., ST. P., & P. "Your grandpa was our friend," said Mrs. Humphrey to Winona. "Don't she look like Ulysses, papa?"

They had only lived in their house four months, but it smelled the way Beryl remembered the Hingham house.

"What's that?" Winona stared at a cage.

"That's our squirrel, Nutty. Came with us from Hingham, Mass.—"

Nutty jumped on the wheel in his cage and rode fast to nowhere.

"He smells," said Winona.

Mrs. Humphrey was interested. "How does he smell, dear?"

"Warm like wax that's been around too long. That's how the beeswax in Mrs. Brigham's sewing bag smells."

The squirrel rode his wheel, ate nuts, and looked distracted. The captain's smile faded. "He's like me. He liked it better near salt water."

"Oh, pa, he don't give a snap for salt water." Mrs. Humphrey put her arm around Beryl and turned to her daughter. "She's a link with our wandering past, Mabel." She led the way into the dining room. "Pa likes it back east talking to his cronies about heading round the Cape and into the China Sea. Mabel and I had enough."

Mabel nodded. She seemed as dried up as the autumn leaf blowing by the window.

At the head of the table sat the captain on his ship's chair that swiveled and was nailed to the floor. In Wabasha there wasn't a deck to roll, but the captain was used to having his chair nailed down, so he nailed it through the carpet that they had bought in Karachi, had used in Hingham, and now covered their western floor. Across the back of the chair, a sailor had carved, "Captain Barnacle."

Going home on the C.M., ST. P., & P., Winona lay down with her head in Beryl's lap. "Has Grandpa White got a squirrel, mama?"

"I don't think so."

"Do you like people with squirrels?"

"Not necessarily. Go to sleep."

15

Dear Aunt Eva, Thank you for that book. I read it twice and I think it's fine. For my birthday I got 33 presents.

Respectfully,
Winona Lloyd

The letter was written on her new notepaper. On it was a picture of a little Dutch girl in a lace-trimmed, pink-flowered dress and cap. Over the dress was a white apron out of which she was tossing grain to a brown hen surrounded by six brown chicks. The little girl was out in the yard, but above her head was a framed picture of a windmill on a dyke with a house in front of it. At the side was a fierce black eagle on a fancy red tripod and a yellow shield with some mythical animal.

Beryl's friend Eva Dill, who had stood up with her at her wedding in Green Bay, had sent Winona her first letter paper from San Francisco for her sixth birthday. It was one of her "33 presents." Beryl read the letter. "I thought you only got sixteen."

"Oh, did I? Well, I'll write her that another time. I don't want to waste a piece of good paper just to tell the truth, do I?"

16

WINONA STOOD outside the bedroom door and listened. In the kitchen Beryl and Mrs. Brigham were getting the pinfeathers out of tomorrow's turkey.

"In Weymouth mama made a big thing out of Thanksgiving," Beryl said.

"Oh, Charlie and I did, too. I'm glad I asked George Snowden to come tomorrow."

Winona went back to the bedroom. From the bureau she took her penny bank, shaped like a schoolhouse painted light brown with red windows and a slit for pennies in the chimney. She gave it a cautious rattle, one ear cocked in the direction of the kitchen. The voices continued. She gave it a shake, a swift upward motion, and a penny flew out the chimney, sped under the bureau. She put the bank down and listened. The voices had taken no notice. Crawling under the bureau, she unlodged the penny from the back caster.

"Mama!" she called.

"Kitchen!"

Winona slid the penny under the hall rug and wandered in. "I might go out. I don't know if I will or not."

Mrs. Brigham pointed to the turkey. "When George sits down to dinner he'll know he chose us a fine bird."

"Um." Winona went back to the hall, put on her coat. For safekeeping she put the penny in her mouth. Once out on Sanburn Street, she skipped round Mrs. Morrison's and the Holbrooks'. Mrs. Holbrook was coming out the door. She was old-looking.

"Hello, Winona."

"Hello." Winona skipped down the hill to Brook Street. The Chinaman on the corner was blowing into the thing that squirted water on the shirt he was ironing.

In front of the Elite Market, George was loading the big wagon. "Want a ride?"

"Maybe. If I don't, I'll see you tomorrow." The bakeshop next door offered sweet buns with juicy black currants, sugar frosting, one penny each. Maybe.

Round on Station Street, Mrs. Grant's Dry Goods had a penny china doll, but at home where would she say she got the penny? She walked by Holbrook's Hardware Store and Mr. Hardy's with the rings in the window, Boynton and Reynolds's grocery store, Backus's grocery store, Mr. McGrath's plumbing store, Mr. Little's tobacco and magazines and newspapers store. And at Ferguson's candy kitchen in the old boarded-up Winona Hotel, she stopped, looked thoughtful and went in. At the counter a girl and a man were having hot chocolate in thick mugs. Two oil stoves were burning. Ferguson's smelled old like Captain Humphrey's squirrel, but they had good candy. A frying pan with bright orange candy, a tin spoon stuck into it, that mama would never let her eat, but today, who would know? The bright orange candy made her feel guilty for taking her penny, her eye then caught a big white peppermint mama liked her to choose. She handed over the wet penny.

On the front seat of George's wagon she ate the peppermint that would get no praise. Praise was sweet and so was the forbidden candy. The peppermint was fair.

17

AFTER DUSTY deserted Glorieta, Winona loved Station Street, looking in the store windows. In Mr. Hardy's was a string of branch coral, a string of shiny gold beads lying on black velvet. Would she choose a signet ring engraved *W L* like Florence Swenson's engraved *F S?* Center front was a tray of rings set with birthstones. Fourteen-carat gold prongs clutched the small turquoise to celebrate December. A fireless opal for October, a bloodstone as big as a cinder, penalty of birth in March. For June, an amethyst that she didn't want. April was a diamond. She looked at her hand. A diamond would look nice.

Holbrook's Hardware Store had two windows with everything in them, including the kitchen sink. A gray soapstone one. Pots, pans, flyswatters, sticky flypaper, custard cups, ink, a snow shovel, a coal hod, a ladder, a broom, a doormat, a carving knife, an eggbeater, nails, tacks, hammer, rope for clothesline, rope for a bundle, rope for enough to hang yourself like the man in *Grimm's Fairy Tales*. Set tubs, a monkey wrench, white or yellow house paint, paint brushes and brushes to scrub, polish for silver, polish for stoves, glue, paste, a camp stool, a pulley, a weathervane, a scraper to put outside the door to scrape mud off, a set of lightning rods like on Dr. Jensen's house. In front, against the window was a painting by Mr. Holbrook's old wife: a boy and a girl holding hands on the foreground of sand the color of johnny-cake, their white faces turned toward a broad strip of blue with a strip of uneven white. A balloon on a string coming out of each of their mouths. "What are the wild waves saying, sister?" the boy was saying.

"That J. S. Holbrook sells the best Blue Flame oil stoves in Winona," the girl was saying.

Mr. Holbrook stood looking out his door. "Hello. You like maple sugar?"

"Yes."

"I got a box in here." He held out his hand. "Let's see where it is. Oh, I know, it's in my office." His office was in the back of the store. He held her hand and walked over to the big rolltop desk, sat down on the big chair in front of it, lifted Winona up on his lap. "We'll find it. Do you want to reach in back of those papers? It's in there." It was a big desk. She leaned way forward. Her short skirt started to raise up. Mr. Holbrook ran his hand softly over her white cotton bottom. "Can you find it?"

Winona wondered, was it right to let Mr. Holbrook touch her drawers?

"Reach further," he said. "I put it there. It's in wax paper."

It probably was all right, he and Mrs. Holbrook and their boys lived around the corner. She stretched her arm in back of some envelopes. Mr. Holbrook's hand left her bottom and went up the front of her drawers. She jumped. It wasn't a tickle, but it was *like* a tickle. Just then she touched the square of wax paper.

"I have it!"

His rough finger stayed where it was. "Take the paper off and give me a little."

Should she tell him not to? But he was giving her his candy. Was it wrong to let him? She broke off a piece.

"That's yours," he said "Give me a small one."

His finger was rough, why did she like how it felt?

"A little piece. Put it in my mouth." She turned to put it in and all at once was lying in his arms. His finger was still there. "Put it in my mouth."

Should she say something? She reached up, he opened his mouth, and before she could put it in, he put his mouth on hers, put his tongue in, then moved it out.

"I took some of your maple sugar. Put mine in my mouth and then taste it." He held her close to his face.

"I have to go home," she said.

It had felt good, then scary.

Mr. Holbrook put her down, straightened her skirt. She didn't say good-bye or anything, just walked past all the set tubs, the oil stoves, out onto Station Street. Is that what Mr. Barney had been doing to Nita Macchi? Why was everything suddenly different? Or maybe it wasn't.

Next door, looking in Mrs. Grant's window were her mother and Mrs. Brigham. Should she walk by as though she didn't see them? Should she tell them where Mr. Holbrook put his hand?

"Hello, darling." It was her mother.

Mrs. Brigham had her eyes on the window. "You like that tea apron, Beryl?"

Should she have another secret?

"I can copy it." Beryl studied the dotted swiss laid out beside the blue Turkish slippers with pom-poms.

Winona suddenly put her arms around her mother's waist and squeezed hard. Probably when you get older you have secrets.

"Those sunbonnet twins are nice, Winona." Mrs. Brigham pointed to a little framed picture beside a card wound with black soutache braid. Propped against Clark's ONT thread was the big cardboard Corticelli cat wound round with plenty of thread. Embroidery hoops held a linen doily with floss to scallop its border and work the wreath of strawberries. McCall's patterns flanked Butterick's and Delineator patterns.

Beryl and Mrs. Brigham discussed veiling with and without chenille dots. Flies went round and round, banged into the glass window pane, slowed down, stunned, then picked up speed and got back on their course. So did Winona. "Mama, when can I get a new hair ribbon?" Secrets fell out of her thoughts and memories. Her eyes were on the roll of three-inch yellow taffeta ribbon that would look beautiful on her red hair.

Mrs. Watson walked into the store. The ladies said, "How do?" with no warmth in it. Mrs. Watson was married to a conductor on the express train to Minneapolis. Their boy was in the third grade at school. Something different about Mrs. Watson.

"Mama, how old do I have to be to have *my* dress fit tight?"

"You want to wear a corset from under your arms," asked Mrs. Brigham, "to right down to your knees and have it pinch you all the time?"

"Mrs. Watson has silk stockings. When I grow up I'm going to have silk stockings and pink satin garters with bows."

"Where does she get such ideas, Beryl?"

"I want to look great like Mrs. Watson and have everybody look at me." Suddenly she thought of Mr. Holbrook. Would Mr. Holbrook want to touch Mrs. Watson there? Would Mrs. Watson like it?

18

WINONA RAN UP the stairs, sniffed the front hall. "Why does the house smell funny?"

"Soap," said Mrs. Brigham.

"Pee-yoo!" She turned up her pretty nose. "Why don't we buy at Larkin's? They give prizes. Mrs. Emery got a magic lantern."

"If I asked Mrs. Carlson to wash with Larkin's soap she wouldn't come anymore."

"Ours smells."

"It smells like what it is: lye and potash and good fat off our Sunday roast."

"I hate fat."

"Well, don't eat it, but don't turn up your nose at our soap. Do you want your rosebud dimity to fade out so it's all white? Your drawers to shrink so you can't sit down?"

Winona went out on the upstairs porch, lay down on the hammock. Over in the Holbrook backyard the Holbrook boys were tossing a ball. She thought of their father touching her drawers. Did *they* do that?

19

THE DOOR to the second grade opened.

"Children, this is Rachel Dudley," said Miss Cameron. "Come in, dear, and take that desk back of Winona. Hold your hand up, Winona."

Winona held her hand up and a little girl with long hair almost as red as Winona's and a face with freckles walked toward the empty seat. Across the aisle, Lawrence Dineen stuck his foot out. Rachel's face turned bright pink under her freckles as she fell into her seat.

"Lawrence, did you mean to do that?" asked Miss Cameron.

"Nope."

"Nope, what?"

"Nope, ma'am."

Outside, snowflakes were coming down so prettily, and maybe Lawrence was telling the truth. Winona turned around and smiled at the new girl. Anyone new was interesting, and she had never seen anyone else but her mother with red hair.

"I'll show you what to do at recess," she whispered.

They went out into the snowflakes. Winona pointed to the big granite wall. "Up there's where I live, the yellow house with the upstairs porch. Where do you?"

"Twenty-six Balch Street."

"Oh, across the tracks. The hill's the best place. But I'll come down to see you."

Saturday morning she crossed the Western Avenue footbridge over the C.M., ST.P., & P. tracks, showed up at 26 Balch Street. Rachel and her sister Kitty, who was in third grade, took her over to Verna Murray's to build a snowman in the Murrays' empty lot. Watching them was a ragamuffin child in an old coat so long it dragged in the snow. On the back of her head was a man's hat. Verna said she came over from the swamp near the Soldiers' Home. Her name was Beazy Noonan and she smelled bad. She didn't ask to play.

The Dudley girls' little sister, Honoria, came looking for them. She was four years old, a flower for a face, soft blonde curls, blue eyes. The Dudley girls loved to show her off. For the first time, Winona wished *she* had a baby sister to show off. She would talk to her mother about it. And even more than their little sister, she wished for Rachel and Kitty's bamboo bookcase up in their room with The Little Colonel series, all the Betty Wales, *When Patty Went to College* and the rest of the Patty books. Rachel let Winona borrow one, but wouldn't it be nice if somebody gave her a bamboo case of her own?

The Dudley girls had their own room, Honoria had hers, and their mother and father slept in one room like Winona and mama.

On Rachel's bureau was a white brush and comb and mirror and shoehorn with *RD* on it in navy blue. On Kitty's bureau was the same with a blue *KD.* Also, things that Rachel said was her manicure set. Her Auntie Belle had given it to her for her fingernails.

What was a manicure? Everybody Winona knew cut their fingernails with scissors, but Auntie Belle told Rachel she should file them with a thing called an emery board or she would never have lovely hands. Besides the emery board there was a small stick of wood the shape of a big toothpick. It said "genuine orangewood stick." There was an article with a chamois skin over it for polishing and a jar of red paste that smelled like the orange candy in the frying pan, a box of white powder marked "Requa's Polish" to powder your nails before you used the chamois polisher. Winona was captivated by such elegance.

"I *love* your white brush and mirror," she said.

"Auntie Belle's friend, Mr. Runnells, gave them to us Christmas and birthdays and every Christmas and birthday he gives us another thing to go with it, and Mr. Hardwick gives us each a five-dollar gold piece. Mr. Hardwick is a lovely man, Auntie Cora is his secretary."

The two-family house at 26 Balch was like everybody's. The Dudley girls' mother was like everybody, pretty with no-particular-colored hair smoothed down, gold spectacles, a sweet voice and a jaunty spirit. She did her housework and seemed as if she enjoyed it. Everything was the same at the Dudleys' except that Honoria was prettier than any child in town and nobody was ever asked to stay to lunch or supper or spend the night. It made Rachel so different Winona chose her for her closest friend.

20

"It must be nearly two, here comes Mrs. Watson. Did I water the Boston fern?" Mrs. Brigham straightened the parlor curtains.

Winona watched Mrs. Watson walk blithely along Sanburn Street, her hourglass figure cuddled into an Alice blue snug-fitting wool suit. Her pointed black patent leather toes and French heels stepped lightly on the maple blossoms that flecked the sidewalk. Her hat was a flowerbed of daisies and roses, veiled by a white dotted chenille veil that caught the breeze blowing across the river. Mrs. Watson's face was pink and white, artificial as the daisies and roses, and both bespoke a good time. Her eyes were bluer than the December turquoise in Mr. Hardy's birthstone ring but unlike the turquoise, Mrs. Watson's blue eyes sparkled, lips red and smiling. Every Tuesday and Thursday afternoon she walked blithely downhill to the Winona Station to catch the C.M., ST.P., & P. 2:10. Every Tuesday and Thursday rich old Mr. Drake was on the train, going to his company's meeting in Minnie. Mr. Watson, the conductor, had his wife sit beside Mr. Drake.

"Why?" asked Winona.

"A lot of things in this world better not to explain. Besides, where would Mr. Dudley get the money to buy that baby blue broadcloth coat with the white fox collar and muff?" Mrs. Brigham said.

"It comes from Bailey's where Mrs. Pillsbury goes."

"But Mr. Pillsbury isn't exactly bookkeeper in his brother's threadworks."

"Well, probably their Auntie Cora gives Honoria things, or Mr. Hardwick, that Auntie Cora is the secretary of."

"Did I water the Boston fern?"

21

"YOU CERTAINLY see a lot of babies, so if a stork brings them wouldn't you see some?" asked Winona. A hot August sun beat down on four girls swinging their lunchboxes. They had reached the woodsy place between the Winona railroad station and the old mansion that had been closed for years.

"My cousin says a baby comes out of a lady's stomach," said Louise cautiously.

Winona rocked with laughter. Marian Brown laughed almost as hard. "A girl at the Greenleaf School says the doctor brings them."

Rachel didn't laugh, she just walked on.

George Snowden's wagon rattled along Hammond Street. He waved.

"Does your mother like Mr. Snowden?" asked Marian. "My cousin Zilpha says she does. Does she?"

"Of course. George is my closest friend . . . Where would the doctor get them?"

"How many will you have, Winona?"

"I may be going to be a nun. I've got the altar for it."

Rachel looked astonished. "I'm your best friend and I never saw it."

"Nobody does. It's in our attic we share with the Chapmans, only they never go up. It was a bureau the Chapmans don't want, but now it's an altar with purple crepe paper over it, hanging down at both sides and lace doilies that're too mended so we don't use them, and a picture of our Lord Jesus Christ with a birchbark cross I made and two white candles in candlesticks."

Marian was fascinated. "How did you think to?"

"Quo Vadis."

"What?"

"It's a book of my mother's that says a girl named Poppeia looked at her own breasts and—"

"Winona!" gasped Rachel, and her freckles stood out against the rush of pink to her cheeks.

Marian stuck to the subject. "What's that got to do with an altar?"

Winona knew the answer. "She prayed a lot. Did I tell you Miriam Hubbard has a grown-up brother that's wife shows her breasts when Miriam says to? Miriam told her to show 'em to her and me. It was in the afternoon in the Hubbards' kitchen."

Rachel clapped her hands over her ears. "That's the most disgusting thing I ever heard!"

Marian thought about it. "She's probably insane."

"If you say I told you, I'll say you took all your clothes off in front of Lawrence Dineen."

Rachel's face turned even pinker. "Winona, please don't be so disgusting."

"Could you have a baby just wishing for it?" asked Louise.

"I thought you were going to say, 'Could you have a baby just taking your clothes off in front of a boy?'" Winona laughed at her own humor.

So did Louise and Marian. And even Rachel.

22

MR. HOLBROOK on his bicycle was starting out from the driveway of his house. Louise and Winona were coming home from school.

"Want to get your bikes and ride over to where there's a whole field I know of daisies? We could pick a bunch to bring home."

"I'll get my bike," said Louise, and rushed across the street to her house.

"Me, too." Winona had the scary feeling, but what

had that to do with daisies?

They followed Mr. Holbrook's bicycle down Sewell Street, past the pines to the meadow.

"I love daisies!" said Louise.

"Me, too. In Glorieta, where I came from, they never heard of one."

They lay their bicycles down and started picking. Mr. Holbrook sat on the stump of a tree and let his bicycle rest next to him. Winona, arms full of daisies, came over. "How can we ride a bicycle and carry these?"

"I'll tie them on the handlebars. Let me see yours." She sat down on his knee. He looked at the daisies on her lap and put his hand under her skirt. His rough thumb went where it had surprised her. With the daisies in her lap, if Louise should turn around, she wouldn't notice.

With his other hand Mr. Holbrook held the daisies. The rough thumb was gentle, didn't hurt, why did she love it? How long ago was it when she didn't know and thought Mr. Barney was tickling Nita Macchi? Now she knew what Mr. Barney had been doing. Did Mr. Barney's thumb feel rough? If she had gone to his garage and implement store for the birthday present, would he have put his hand there?

23

EVERY WEDNESDAY afternoon the Dudley girls' aunts came out from Minneapolis on the 3:30 train. With them was Auntie Belle's friend, Mr. Runnells. Winona loved to see the three stroll away from the station. Mr. Runnells, perfectly tailored, and matching his elegance were Auntie Cora and Auntie Belle, blonde hair marcelled like the pictures in *Bon Ton* magazine, their clothes the latest fashion. Winona thought they looked readier to go to Mrs. Pillsbury's than to visit a two-family house across the tracks on shabby Balch Street.

"Winona!" Rachel rushed up the wide stairs of Number Forty-one. "Auntie Cora and Auntie Belle are going to let me bring you to lunch on Saturday!"

"That's the day you're coming with George and me to pick out our furniture," said Beryl.

"Mama, how did I know Auntie Cora and Auntie Belle were going to ask me? Mama, will my gray silk with the pink stripes be finished?"

Her excitement lasted right up to when she and Rachel and Kitty walked down the finest residential street in Minneapolis and went into an imposing yellow brick building as elegant as Auntie Cora and Auntie Belle.

The front door of their apartment was opened by a maid, and through French blue velvet portieres, polished mahogany caught the light from the tall windows framed with French blue velvet curtains and Brussels lace. Velvet chairs and couches stood on the soft-colored Persian carpet, and everywhere were pretty things that looked expensive.

The luncheon table cover was lace. A silver bowl, frothing with hothouse daffodils, stood in the center, surrounded by delicate china, more silver and crystal. The food was like Sunday. After lunch Auntie Belle told the girls to say good-bye to Auntie Cora. She was taking them to a matinee at the Orpheum Vaudeville Theatre.

Back at Sanburn Street Winona recounted every minute to her mother and Mrs. Brigham and George, who was staying for supper.

"Then the Auntie Cora's hired girl put cut-glass bowls with water and a geranium leaf down on a plate in front of each of us and Auntie Cora and the Auntie Belle put their fingers in and washed across their mouths." Her eyes were starry. "Even every little thing was beautiful and expensive."

"Don't you want to ask what George and I got for your room? Why are you so impressed with bowls of water?"

Mrs. Brigham nodded. "We had finger bowls when Charlie and I had company at our house on Prospect. They're nice, but they're nothing."

Winona looked far away to the yellow brick apartment house. *"Everything* there is beautiful and that's how I'm going to have *my* things."

"Well, is that a reason to look at us as though you didn't like us? George got a great present for you."

"What is it?"

"Never mind."

She'd shared this day and now she wouldn't share with anyone. On the *surface* she'd share with mama and Mrs. Brigham and George, but what she really thought, what she was after, she'd keep to herself. Auntie Belle and Auntie Cora had everything expensive and didn't do anything for it. Auntie Cora was Mr. Hardwick's secretary, but she went away all summer and came out to Balch Street all Wednesday afternoon. Who worked for Mr. Hardwick then?

24

BERYL CAME out of their bedroom, stood by the stairs that Mr. Waldemar said were wide. She'd changed from the light blue silk wedding dress to a light blue suit she and Mrs. Brigham had made and trimmed with an organdy jabot bought at Mrs. Grant's. Her face was the color of a June rose.

"Gee!" George sounded almost reverent. "Isn't she a picture?"

Mrs. Brigham turned to Winona. Winona, looking far older than her twelve years, stared at her mother. Beryl went over to her. "Darling, you look after things, huh?"

A little of the rose had gone. Winona didn't answer.

"We'll scrape along all right." Mrs. Brigham put her arm around Winona's shoulder. Beryl sat down in the hall chair, bought that first trip to Minneapolis.

"Look, baby, every day I'll send you a postcard for the album, and we'll be thinking about you all the—"

"No, you won't." Winona's voice was cold as a stone at the bottom of the Brook Street brook.

"Sure we will." George sounded anxious. "And we'll bring you a grand present. What do you want us to bring you?"

Winona looked at him. "Money."

"Winona." Beryl put her hand out to her. No response.

"Good idea. We'll see what the money looks like in other places and bring it back for you to compare."

No response. The Congregational clock struck five. Mrs. Brigham made a little sign.

"Good-bye, baby," said Beryl. "I love you."

Winona didn't relax.

"You go," said Mrs. Brigham. "We two will do fine."

"So long, Winona." George didn't risk a hug. "She's your mother first, and then somewhere after that, *I* come in."

No response.

"Do your part, darling, or nothing will work." Beryl's arms still around her. She looked at the stern little face. Mrs. Brigham gave another sign. Beryl kissed Winona, gave Mrs. Brigham a hug, and they were gone. Through the open window the sound of Mike Dineen's station hack as it rattled around onto Wabasha Street down the hill to the station. How empty the hall was.

"I suppose you and I could do worse than pick up a little. The question is, where to start?"

Winona studied her coldly. "I've got something to do."

"Anything *I* could join in? I feel kind of lost."

"No, you don't. You just want to ladle out sympathy I don't want. I want my father and my father's dead. What can you do about that? My mother went off with the grocery man."

"Winona!"

"You got us to come here. It's *you* made this terrible thing happen."

"Maybe it won't be terrible."

Winona laughed scornfully. *"Face* things."

Mrs. Brigham thought a minute. "What would be best for you?"

"To stand it by myself."

"Maybe think about some of the rest of the human race. Think about how bad *I* feel. You and your mother won't be living here with me any more."

"You feeling bad is all that lets me bear it."

Mrs. Brigham went into the kitchen and closed the door.

If Mrs. Brigham had fought back, that might have brought relief. Instead, she was alone with the stairs her mother had gone down looking happy. Rage surged up. She turned away from the stairs that had made her suffer and went into the room that this morning was still hers and her mother's. On the bed was Beryl's wedding dress, lying softly where her mother had slept last night. Now she was laughing with George and when it got dark, sleeping with him on the train. Would he be naked like Mr. Swenson when Florence saw him come out of her mother's room? Would he touch her mother where Mr. Holbrook touched her? Was that what her mother wanted?

The closet door was open. On pegs were her mother's clothes, not like the pale blue silk wedding dress that belonged to the one who left her. The brown skirt on the peg was what her mother wore. The black skirt, the long blue serge coat, the old petticoat, the old corset on the chair, the blue bedroom slippers worn at the sides and the pom-poms raveled. The black boots, muddy from yesterday, when she and her mother walked home from school through the spring mud. They were her mother's, not the new patent leather she'd gone down the wide stairs in. That was George's wife who had gone down the stairs and what she had *really* meant to say was, "Baby, smile, please *like* to lose your mother."

And George: "She'll always be your mother."

Did he think he could buy her off with a present?

"Money." That must have cut. That showed where he stood with her. Her mother he'd got, but he hadn't got *her*. And the first one to call him her father, she'd—Suddenly, she was down on the closet floor, face pressed against the muddy shoes, weeping. Yesterday, arm in arm, they'd walked home in the rain, under the black umbrella, they'd walked home. Now where was home? Why hold onto it? No one else had. All her mother wanted was for her to act nice while George touched her place and did things to her. She snatched up the mud-crusted shoes and rubbed them on the pale blue silk dress.

25

MOVING DAY. George and Beryl would get back late that afternoon and go right to their new home. Forty-one Maplewood Avenue.

"You go over to Rachel's and when it's lunchtime, bring her back. You'll be the first to eat in the new house." Mrs. Brigham waited for a little encouragement. Winona walked down the stairs.

"You're welcome," Mrs. Brigham called after, then felt sorry. Winona wasn't behaving well and that wasn't a happy state. Mr. Chapman with his wagon was going to pick up Winona's bed, bureau, books, dolls and clothes. Beryl and George had bought all new furniture. Mr. Roney and she and Buster had placed it where they thought the new couple must have meant it to go.

Forty-one Maplewood Avenue was a two-family house like on Sanburn Street, but each family had two stories and an attic. Mr. and Mrs. Roberts, who owned it, lived on the Anderson Street side, and rented 41 Maplewood. It was in the part of town called "down on the plains."

At Sanburn Street, Mr. Chapman walked up the stairs, looked mournfully around him, took off his old derby and studied Winona's bed. "I'll get this apart. Good you got wide stairs."

Mrs. Brigham nodded. "Then if you tackle the bureau, Mr. Chapman, I'll follow with the chair. For the rest of the things, I saved these packing boxes from what we bought in Minnie when we moved in."

"I should hope so. Why throw away good things like them?"

"They'll do for her dolls and books and we'll get her dresses in some more boxes and a suitcase. This old bag's her shoes and underwear, it's called a Gladstone. Don't ask me why."

When they got everything out, it looked lonely. "Pitch in!" she told herself. Her cure for worry was "Pitch in!" She turned the key in the lock. Mr. Chapman pointed to the front seat of his wagon. Pippin clopped along at a leisurely gait and at Number Forty-one Mr. Chapman tethered her to the Winona granite quarry hitching post in front. Mrs. Brigham pointed to the clapboard house painted light gray with the white trim.

"I told Beryl and Winona all the houses here were white with green blinds. Didn't they used to be?"

Mr. Chapman thought it over. "No."

The front porch was narrow, big enough for four chairs, a window in the parlor looked across it, one in the dining room looked on the end, the front door was heavy oak with a big carved metal "41" on the frame, and a handsome brass oval doorknob. When Winona later thought of 41 Maplewood Avenue, she remembered the doorknob.

Mrs. Brigham unlocked the door. This key was just a usual one, not big like Sanburn Street. The floor in the front hall was polished and so were the stairs. Mr. Chapman remarked on the newel post shaped like a pineapple. "A handsome thing."

"When I lived in New Mexico a friend sent me a real pineapple from Honolulu," Mrs. Brigham said. She put the hatrack against the wall. The new table with the brass lamp and red china shade went between the hatrack and the new birch armchair. A wide arch led into the parlor. Beryl had chosen light green paper with silver moiré design. The new cherry oblong table stood in the center with the elaborate brass lamp and Chinese parchment shade, gift of the Tubman Produce Company that George did business with. On the mantle over the pale buff brick fireplace was the marble clock Mrs. Brigham had given them. The black leather armchair had been George's father's. Along the wall where the window looked across the porch was the secondhand piano George had bought for Winona.

The dining room was also repapered. Beryl and Mr. Roberts had chosen a fruit design, bananas and oranges tangled up with apples and melons. The new golden oak oblong dining table had four chairs with black imitation leather seats, two more flanking the reading table by the Maplewood Avenue window. It held a green-shaded gasolier. On the big oak sideboard, cut-glass wedding presents sparkled.

Between the dining room and kitchen was a small entry with stairs to the cellar. Mr. Roberts had put in a new Franklin stove, beyond it was the sink and a Blue Flame oil stove, from Mr. Holbrook's. Looking out on the back lawn two windows rattled when the Minneapolis trains and freights went by. It was a good kitchen and a good pantry. It had a window on Maple-wood Avenue.

Upstairs, George and Beryl's room was on the corner. Anderson Street and Maplewood Avenue. Next to it, all of its four windows on Maplewood, was Winona's room. She'd chosen wallpaper with big yellow roses, and Mrs. Brigham and Beryl had covered a shirtwaist box with yellow flowered chintz. It held dresses, and the top was padded to sit on. Against the wall, Mr. Chapman placed the brass bed Beryl and Winona had slept in up on Sanburn Street. Now it was Winona's alone. The bureau and mirror faced it, beside it was a bamboo book-case, like Rachel's. George had picked it out for her.

At the end of the hall was a small spare room and the bathroom. The floor above was the attic with a slant-ceilinged room on either side. "Good place to hang the wash on a wet day," said Mrs. Brigham.

Mr. Chapman looked around. "Well, we didn't knock a hole in anything." He tipped his hat and went.

Lamb chops for lunch, Winona's favorite. Mrs. Brigham beat the egg whites to go on top of a chocolate floating island. Everything would be all right, it was just Winona's getting used to it. She whisked the eggs out of the bowl onto the chocolate.

What nobody had understood was that Winona didn't know what was going on. They had spoiled her, and she thought George was hers for whenever she needed him. Beryl had told her they were going to get married, but it was just when Winona was thinking about the Mother Goose party Mrs. Emery was giving Louise and was showing Beryl how she wanted her Little Bo Peep cos-tume made. George and Beryl had asked her to come to

Minneapolis with them to pick out the furniture, but that was the day Rachel's aunts had invited her to lunch. George and Beryl even went on the same train, but Winona sat with Rachel and Kitty and that night at supper would only talk about Rachel's aunts. It made Beryl angry. Even the day before the wedding when Winona and Beryl walked home from school, Winona talked about her birthday party and was excited because Anna Whitman said she'd come. But the morning of the wedding, when Beryl was getting ready, Winona turned into a thundercloud. The cloud still hadn't disappeared.

"Yoo-hoo!" The door was flung open. "Here's Rachel!" Winona was radiant. Mrs. Brigham's heart leaped. "I'm starving. We'll be right down." She put her arm around Rachel and ran her up the stairs. "Don't you adore yellow roses? I have four windows and I'm going to have a table in the corner with a cocoa pot and cups and saucers so I can entertain."

Rachel looked at the bamboo bookcase. "That's a dandy."

"Oh, I said I wouldn't live here if they didn't get it. I adore bamboo. Did I tell you Anna Whitman said she'd come to my birthday party? I adore her. Come see the dining room. It's got adorable wallpaper, not like that old frowsy Sanburn Street. Did I tell you 'frowsy' is my new word? Don't you adore it?"

"Ready, girls." Mrs. Brigham whisked the breaded lamb chops onto two plates.

26

ANNA INVITED Winona to spend her thirteenth birthday at Lake Minnetonka.

The Whitmans had a cottage and Anna and Winona and Mrs. Whitman were alone there in the daytime, but Mr. Whitman and his friend Mr. Wilson came in time for dinner. Mr. Wilson was a stockbroker in Minneapolis, a bachelor, and had a room at the Whitmans' for the summer. After dinner Anna played the piano and Winona did the new dances, sometimes crazy, improvised ones. Mr. and Mrs. Whitman sat out on the porch or strolled along the lakefront, but Mr. Wilson applauded Winona. Sometimes she whirled around so that Mr. Wilson could see her drawers. Why was that exciting? He was just a pleasant, middle-aged man, maybe older than middle-aged, well-to-do.

Further along the shore at the resort hotel, in the Palm Garden Restaurant, they had a cabaret show. Winona had never seen a cabaret. "I'm dying to go!"

"But it's night," said Anna.

"I'm dying to. It sounds wicked."

"But how could we?"

"Mr. Wilson, do you go to cabaret shows?" Winona

smiled at him. Could she make him take them? "The star of this one is May Yohe. She's a London musical comedy star. I read she was married to Lord Hope that had the Hope diamond. She's only appearing there one week."

"At the Palm Garden Cabaret?" Mr. Wilson was surprised.

"Aren't you dying to see her? May Yohe! She must be someone who will steal your heart."

Mr. Wilson said he didn't think so, but he'd like to take the girls if Mrs. Whitman would come. Mr. Whitman was going away on a two-day business trip and Mrs. Whitman thought it would be a lovely idea. Everybody dressed up and walked down the shore to the Palm Garden in the North Star Hotel. Mr. Wilson ordered a splendid dinner starting with caviar. He asked Mrs. Whitman if he might order champagne.

What excitement! What a letdown! Winona's first champagne tasted sour, not like she had imagined, and the caviar tasted like salty sardines, only sardines were better. Expensive tastes take time, but she'd get them. "Don't you *love* caviar?" she said.

A fanfare from the orchestra, the spotlight picked up a matronly figure in bright silver and blue form-fitting brocade, nothing as sexy as Mrs. Watson. What had she looked like when she caught the fancy of Lord Hope and wore his diamond? They said anybody wore it had bad luck, did wearing it make May Yohe look too heavy? Why didn't she keep looking good? She'd gotten there, how did she lose the knack? She sang five numbers. The response was tepid.

That night Winona lay in bed wide awake long after Anna went to sleep. Mr. Wilson was pleasant, looked all right, bought champagne, caviar, had seen her drawers. What if she let him keep her? Did that mean go to bed with him whenever he said to? Let him see her with all her clothes off when he said to? Would he have her live in his apartment or fix up an apartment where he would come to do it to her? Would he give her money? He wouldn't be ideal but he could get her away from living in Winona. Of course, she'd only get to Minneapolis. What if he wanted to marry her? Perish the thought! Probably at first she wouldn't be good doing it, but people said she was a beauty and she'd learn how. Beauty and doing it great would have to get her everything expensive, like with Auntie Cora and Auntie Belle.

27

WINONA WAS looking at the pink satin ribbon in Mrs. Grant's store window.

"Want to walk down to see my new horse?" Mr. Holbrook walked briskly, Winona beside him. "She's black and handsome." They walked past Mrs. Grant's, Mr. Hardy's, down Station Street.

What if she was walking to see Mr. Wilson's new horse? Would Mr. Wilson touch her there like Mr. Holbrook was going to? They passed Brazee Hall on the corner where she went to Miss Burns's class in dancing and deportment. They passed Maplewood. They walked to Butler's Pond. Near it was Mr. Holbrook's stable. The new black horse was a beauty. Winona patted her head.

"She'll draw my carriage nice. We'll go for a ride one day." He helped her up to the big cushioned seat then got up beside her, took her hand and put it inside the front of his trousers. He lifted her skirt, unbuttoned her drawers, and all at once the front of him was pushing where his thumb had hurt. It felt scarier than anything she'd done. His hand was where her breasts were starting. Was this what people did to live in beautiful apartments like Auntie Cora's and Auntie Belle's? Did Mr. Runnells do this to Auntie Belle? Did she like it? Did it hurt her?

Mr. Holbrook pushed harder, then shuddered and moved away quickly.

"You run along," he said, and got down from the carriage.

Was this the way Mr. Wilson would do when he took off her drawers in the apartment he got for her to stay in?

28

Mr. holbrook was old. Wouldn't boys do it better? No use to think of any she knew. No one was rich or probably would be, but there were a lot of rich girls in Winona who must have brothers or maybe whose father was a widower and would like to marry young. The rich girls went to Mrs. Weldon's Private School for Girls on Spruce Avenue towards the bluff. Anna Whitman was a day pupil and through her eyes Winona saw the life she dreamed about.

Mrs. Weldon's school stood for the things heaven was against. Heaven was where not to feel above one's brother, but at Mrs. Weldon's everybody was above everybody who didn't go to Mrs. Weldon's. Why did heaven tout everybody off worldly goods? Was heaven a place maybe for people who couldn't get anywhere?

On Sundays the girls filed into church, chaperoned by a teacher, lest harm befall them between Spruce Avenue and the service. Winona waited outside. Sometimes when she waited Mr. and Mrs. Holbrook passed by and the two Holbrook boys. Mr. Holbrook and Mrs. Holbrook said hello to Winona, and Winona said hello. Then the girls from Mrs. Weldon's school would pass and, with luck, she found a seat in the pew behind Geraldine Van der Linder, a young princess from Chicago's Gold Coast. Did Geraldine Van der Linder have a brother?

The backs of Mrs. Weldon's girls' elegant suits and coats bespoke life where price wasn't important, just the cut.

Next to Geraldine, Winona admired Alice Glover, who Anna said was in the graduating class. June would see her ready to take her place in Sioux City, Iowa, society. The pink-frilled white-gloved hand handled Alice's personal prayer book, and when Winona practiced at home with *Quo Vadis* why couldn't she achieve that same worldly sophisticated ease? She held *Quo Vadis* upended on her lap, elbow resting on it, chin resting on the palm of her hand. Why couldn't she capture Alice Glover's elegance? Could a man go crazy over elegance? Would Alice have love affairs or would she be a debutante that wouldn't do it until she got married?

Another pupil Winona admired was Helen Sears, who lived with her family a block away from Mrs. Weldon's gates, corner of Spruce Avenue and Willow Street. Mr. Sears, slender, elegant, wore a Du Maurier pointed gray beard and was blind. Helen's brother was handsome, important in New York, and once in a while came back to see the family.

Poetic-looking young Helen with brown hair, violet eyes set wide apart, had a voice with a sniff that sounded as though she were forever starting a cold. What would it be if Winona learned to talk and look like her? Maybe not look like her but talk like her. Winona liked her own looks. Helen dismissed the state of Minnesota, all the fun, she said, was in Milwaukee, where in the autumn she was entering New Downer College. For seeing everybody that was anybody she recommended lunching at Milwaukee's Pfister Hotel. What spectacular names Mrs. Weldon's girls knew! Pfister Hotel! Sioux City! Chicago! If she had to stick to the truth, all she could work into the conversation was Glorieta, and Minneapolis, which Helen said was not fashionable. A good rule might be stick to the truth if the truth held some interest, otherwise why not throw in a Sioux City or Milwaukee or even a trip to New York? If you weren't born with the gift of luck, acquire it. Until then, what about making it up?

Would Helen's brother be going to get married? Would he want to marry Winona? Would she want to marry him? And have babies? Why have babies? No babies, she wanted to be the one. That was no lie.

29

OF A DIFFERENT kind of elegance, Winona was dazzled by the married daughter of old lady Mahler, who lived over at the foot of Garvin Bluff. Her spinster daughter, Miss Ida, lived with her and from time to time the afternoon train from Minnie brought the former Lily Mahler, a blonde beauty married to a rich Chicagoan whose family owned all the milk in Illinois. Lily had married Frank Corey to get out of Winona, though that wasn't what she told *him.* Her mother and Ida had to have a meal ticket and when Lily married Frank Corey that took care of that. She sent them the money every first of the month and forgave them. Frank Corey was nine years older and from time to time went into seclusion with what Lily called his asthma. It left in its wake empty bottles of Green River whiskey.

One look at Lily stepping off the Minneapolis train and Winona thought, how would she scrape up an acquaintance? when it turned out that Anna knew old Mrs. Mahler and Miss Ida.

"Is 'Mahler' foreign?" Winona asked hopefully.

Anna thought about it. "I guess so."

"Where does it sound like from?"

Calling on Miss Ida one afternoon, Winona asked her.

"Oh, we're descended from the Hapsburgs," she said. "Look at Lily, she's pure Viennese, though she's never been nearer Vienna than Chicago."

Winona was enchanted. Perhaps people at the Hotel Pfister looked Viennese. She'd ask Helen Sears, and until then went up to the third floor and privately studied herself. Long red, red hair, white skin like a flower petal, light green eyes the color of—what color were they like? "You're beautiful," she told herself. "Nobody here has eyelashes this long. They say if you cut them they'll grow." Why should she? Hers were perfect. Could she look Viennese? She studied the mirror over the bureau. Could she? Do her hair like Lily's. Did it make her look

Viennese? No Viennese blood in her from Grandpa Ulysses White. Certainly only blue blood from Boston's Commonwealth Avenue Grandfather Lloyd who had written he'd adopt her if she never saw her mother.

She rang up Anna. "Do you think I could look Viennese?"

"Oh, I don't think so."

"Do you think I could look fast?"

"Oh, no."

"Do you think Lily Corey looks fast?"

"She's married."

"That doesn't matter, look at Mrs. Watson."

"Well, that's so."

"I walked all the way behind Lily Corey to the foot of Garvin's Bluff to see her skirt swish. It was dark blue taffeta with huge white polka dots. It swished-swished above her ankles and even Mrs. Watson's silk stockings aren't *that* sheer. Did I tell you she had on black patent leather slippers? Anna, I don't think you can be thinking. Why don't you think she's fast?"

"Well, do *you* think so?"

"You can't say she looks like somebody *married.* Do you think she peroxides her hair? Oh, she *must* be fast, the way she walks, I'll come up and show you."

She went down the hall to Beryl and George's room. Their door was closed.

"Going up to Anna's," she called out. Their door closed still embarrassed her. Her mother and George doing things they didn't want *anyone* to see.

Beryl didn't open the door. "All right," she called out.

What was it they did? Who would tell her how? She ran down the stairs. How could she get married to Mr.

Wilson? Get married or go to bed with him and have a flat of her own? Could she get to know Lily Corey and talk it over with her?

She practiced Lily's walk up Highview Avenue. Anna was waiting on her back steps. "Know what you look like?"

"Fast."

"Nope. Passionate."

"Well, *that's* fast. If you don't want to be a teacher or a secretary or a trained nurse and are passionate, then you're fast."

"You think so?"

"Some man gives you a flat and a maid and clothes and jewelry and you go out to restaurants and theatres and when you come home, he goes to bed with you. Well, don't you have to be passionate?"

"But Lily Corey can't have a man go to bed with her, she's got Mr. Corey."

"But don't you think he probably has to go all over Illinois to visit the Corey Dairies and that's when some man has Lily in a flat."

"What makes you think up things like that?"

"Because I'll probably be in a flat myself."

"Winona!"

"In Minnie or Milwaukee at the Pfister Hotel or even Chicago. I made Miss Ida swear she'd give me a letter to Mrs. Corey if I do."

Anna thought about it. "Couldn't she introduce you here?"

"Here I'd feel funny, I'd feel more like it in Chicago. Maybe George and my mother will ask me again. They asked me once when George had to go buy supplies. Of course, we don't hit it off, but I'd go to Chicago with him to meet Mrs. Corey. You know who might get me a flat? Mr. Wilson?"

"Oh, he's wild about you but not in that way. He lives in the Union Club in St. Paul."

"He's not my ideal."

Anna laughed at the idea. "He's as old as papa."

"I don't mind. I'd have all my bills paid and pearls and diamonds and swell clothes. He told me he thought my hair was beautiful. He's really rich and has a lovely way about him. He's not too old to go to bed with, don't your mother and father?"

"Oh, sure, but I don't think Mr. Wilson would keep you in a flat."

"He'd be putty in my hands. Do you like that expression?"

"He'd have a fit if he heard you talk like this." Anna giggled.

"Don't act like a simp. When you were playing the piano I did high kicks to let him see my drawers. When a man sees a girl's drawers it's suggestive. He thinks if he sees her drawers she'd show him what's under them."

"Winona!"

"When I kicked high, I bet if I asked, 'Want to have a flat for me, Mr. Wilson, in the fashionable part of Minneapolis or I just as soon St. Paul?'—want to bet a quarter he'd say yes?"

30

Decoration day was the Grand Army Parade. Winona wore her rose-colored challis with a high Empire waist she got Beryl to copy from Empress Josephine's picture in *McCall's*. To the Empress dress Winona added wide black velvet ribbon threaded through loops of challis. Her hair ribbons were new, wide black grosgrain from Mrs. Grant's store. She'd had to save up a lot, but admiration more than grosgrain was what she was buying. She didn't look at the parade, she was looking to see who was looking at her. George and Beryl and Mrs. Brigham stood on the Hammond Street curbstone, watching.

"She's growing up, Beryl." Mrs. Brigham pointed to Winona talking prettily to landlord Roberts. "People look at her. She's pretty, y'know. She's going to be a beauty."

George put his arm around Beryl. "I bet your mother said the same about you."

Beryl laughed. So did Mrs. Brigham. All the years and it still was Beryl and Mrs. Brigham. Mr. Farwell's black Packard, loaned to the GAR veterans, rolled slowly past. There were only three veterans now, and one was from East Liberty, old Mr. Perry Lewis.

"I drove him over in the flivver," said his daughter. "But this time's the last. He tells how he's seen General Sherman, but all I know is the ride from East Liberty made him wet his pants. Does Uncle Sam pay the bill for that?"

The car stopped and old Mr. Lewis waved his hand and bowed. So dignified.

"I'll pay," said Mrs. Brigham.

"Oh, save your money. Riding over, I told him, 'Enjoy *this* time because it's no more.' He just yelled something filthy at me. He can get cross as a otter. 'Button your lip,' I says. Y'have to shut him up."

The car started to roll along again. The town's own GAR, Judge Webster, brought back for the day from Mankato Soldiers' Home, offered Mr. Lewis a chew of tobacco. The Winona High School Band marched by playing "Marching Through Georgia." Everybody applauded. The Boy Scouts marched behind it, looking clean and paying attention to the scoutmaster only when they weren't looking to see their mothers. Eagle Scout Larry Dineen searched the crowd for a new girl in town.

The last float went by with Mrs. Emery as the South and Miss Zilpha Brown as the North, arms entwined. Mrs. Brigham applauded. "It was good, I enjoyed it. I'll go over to the cemetery, Beryl."

Beryl and George watched her go through the gate of Mount Winona.

"Why don't I call her Allie?" she said to George.

"Why don't you?"

"Oh, I couldn't."

"Me, neither."

"Mrs. Dunham that works for Burke Sturdevant says

he calls her Mrs. Dunham, and she's been his housekeeper for three years and calls him Burke."

"Gee, Beryl, how did you ever go for me?"

She leaned forward, kissed him full on the lips.

Mr. Perry Lewis's daughter gave them a crabbed look. People wetting their pants, a wife kissing her husband on the mouth in front of everybody, like they were in their room with the door shut. Life was too much.

31

MRS. BRIGHAM put her bunch of snowballs and purple lilacs on the grass in front of the gravestone marked "Charles Brigham." Should she have had the stonecutter make it "Charlie"? When death strikes, no one can think much and the conventional thing gets done. "Charles" on the stone seemed like someone else. He was Charlie. Charlie. All at once her eyes grew moist. Charlie. Feelings last a long time. Charlie.

"Hello."

She looked up. "Why, Joe."

"You brought some out to Charlie, I just left some for Addie."

"Well." She stopped. There was too much to say. And to leave unsaid. When she and Charlie lived in Winona,

Joseph Penniman and Adelaide had lived next door in the old house that Joe's father had built, cinnamon colored with a big cupola. Not grand like the white mansion that Joe built for him and Addie. Stately with grand columns. Why had she thought all the houses were white? Joe and Addie and she and Charlie had been friends, and no matter how grand Mr. and Mrs. Joseph Penniman became, the four had good times together. Then Charlie died and there was no money, they had spent it on living nice. She went out to her brother in Glorieta, and not long after that came a letter saying Addie had passed away and Joe was off to Florida and the Adirondacks. He wrote, "I want to run away from the house she managed so beautifully. I don't care where I'm going or even where I've been."

He looked at her admiringly. "Allie, it's nice to see you, I've been away a lot."

"Me, too, but I had to come back here." She looked at "Charles Brigham." "This is the best place on earth, Joe."

"I went to Florida and Lake George, all over, everywhere you can mention, then I came home. Even without Addie, it's home. Want to walk back? Or ride?"

"I'd like a ride."

They walked out to the main gate, where Joe's brown Packard touring car stood, his chauffeur beside it.

"I'll drive, Vernon," he said. "Hop in, Allie."

She laughed. "So long since anyone's called me Allie, I wondered who you were talking to."

"You're the one." He helped her into the front seat, went round and took the wheel. "In, Vernon."

"Yes, sir."

"Want to go right home or take a spin?"

"Lovely."

"We'll see what the river looks like." He turned the car around. "Have a cup of tea over at Rollingstone? You still like tea?"

"I do. Yes, I *do* . . .".

32

"WINONA!" GEORGE shook the bed.

What was that? She was dreaming of talking to Lily Corey in Chicago.

"Winona, wake up." George never sounded like this. His voice was afraid.

She opened her eyes. "Go quick for Dr. Jensen. Quick! Beryl's sick."

"What?"

"Beryl's sick and Dr. Jensen has to come. I'd go but I have to stay with her."

It was five o'clock in the morning. Only a little bit light. She put a coat on over her nightgown, ran down Maplewood to Fayette, past Mrs. Helmersen's boarding house, past Florence Swenson's, turned onto Brook and crossed Farragut, ran up the steps of Dr. Jensen's house. His office entrance was on the Farragut Street side of his piazza. A bell marked "Night" was by the door. Winona rang it and Dr. Jensen's sleepy voice said, "Yes?" She hadn't noticed an open tube right over the bell.

"It's Winona Lloyd. Mama's sick and George Snowden said to please come quick!"

"You're on Maplewood?"

"Forty-one on the corner."

"You run along, I'll be right there."

How awful to be frightened. Her heart was jumping and her legs felt wobbly, she couldn't run. Dr. Jensen's voice sounded like it was really serious. How quiet Brook Street was. She'd never been outdoors at five in the morning. She'd never been outdoors with trouble.

33

THE MISCARRIAGE had been dangerous, but Dr. Jensen was a fine doctor, and Beryl was getting well. Mrs. Brigham propped her up in bed with two pillows behind her and brought a tray. "Hot chicken broth." Mrs. Josie Emerson had brought over a chicken from East Liberty.

Beryl looked out the window at the maple that in the spring had the red buds. "Remember that hot day Mrs. Macchi brought some? Let's send her a postcard."

"I'll buy one. Get this in you, you got color today. I

85

didn't like that fish-belly white. Did I tell you Annie
Sedig will start tomorrow? You were napping when she
came, she's real lovely. She was hired girl for Mrs. Fenno
and you know Mrs. Fenno. Fussy. And Annie stuck it
out with them three years. She must be a saint."

"Did she like it here?"

Mrs. Brigham nodded. "Of course. And she hasn't
even seen you and George. She said Mrs. Fenno didn't
like her to have company in the kitchen. Eat your soup.
And she's got a sweetheart. I should think she would.
Did I tell you she's pretty? Early December she's getting
married. He's a stonecutter over at the quarry. Swedish,
too, but her getting married is no skin off your behind,
you'll be doing for yourself long before. Can you get
some more down? Annie'll start in the morning."

"Did you tell her George has to get up at six?"

"Five, I said. She didn't care. She's got a lovely smile
and white teeth. Unusual for Swedish is her black curly
hair. You don't see many dark Swedes. And you just
know she's willing and obliging. Did I tell you she has
lovely teeth? She's good all right, I don't plan on telling
her anything more than once. Is that all the soup you can
take?"

Beryl nodded.

"You did fine. Here's custard."

34

"Hurry up, Winona, it isn't good for horses to stand still in this cold and I don't want George kept waiting."

"Mama, you told me a hundred times."

"Well, hundred times yourself downstairs. You, too, Rachel, get a wiggle on. We have to go up to Sanburn Street to pick up Mrs. Brigham."

"I'm hooking her up, Mrs. Snowden. I only have four hooks more, I mean five."

Beryl put out the green-shaded gasolier in the dining room, turned down the wick of the red-shaded brass lamp George's boy at the Elite had given them for their wedding.

"Winona." She hung her coat on the pineapple newel post. "Bring down Annie's wedding present."

"Oh, mama, I'm doing something."

"Oh, excuse me, honeybunch, I'll just run up and down stairs again so as not to disturb you. Bring it and bring it down quick! It's in my room on the bed."

"Nona's hooking *me* up, Mrs. Snowden."

Winona gave Rachel a shove that landed her on the yellow-flowered shirtwaist box. "Don't call me *Nona*— I told you three times!"

"Winona, I mean. Excuse me."

She grabbed the back of Rachel's dress as if she would like to tear it. "If you can't say Winona, go home and never come back again."

"When you get mad your face looks awful. You screw it up."

Beryl shouted up the stairs, "Bring that present for Annie or I'll come up there and tackle the both of you!"

Winona looked over the banisters. "You can't say 'the both of you,' mama."

"Why can't I?"

Rachel held up the present. "I've got it, Mrs. Snowden."

"It's china. Be careful."

Beryl disappeared.

"You looked terrible, but now you look nice again." She followed Winona down the stairs.

Beryl looked at Chalky. "Did I give you your supper, darling?"

"Chalky disgusts me. He's a mutt," Winona said.

"Well, so are we. Lay it on the parlor sofa, Rachel." She gave Chalky a hug. "Don't you listen, darling. Come here and get a nice bone I was saving for soup, but you take it, sweetheart. Winona, put your wool stockings over your—"

"*Yes,* mama!" She rolled her eyes back in her head at the boredom of it.

"Start to get your coats on, George will be—"

"I *abhor* galoshes! I wish I had carriage boots, pearl-gray velvet carriage boots edged with gray squirrel fur from O'Neill, Winston's. Does your Auntie Cora have carriage—?"

Horses' hooves and sleigh bells rang out.

"I'm brazen about it, I'd give my soul for pearl-gray velvet—"

"Here's George!" Beryl's voice sounded different, full of excitement. She flung the front door open. "We're ready!"

Did George give her mother that scary feeling?

Outside, lanterns lit, was the big Elite Market pung.

"George, lovey, we're ready."

Winona looked at her mother aghast. "We're not going in the *pung.*"

"What's wrong with the—"

"Mama, you don't go to a wedding in a grocery delivery pung that says 'Snowden's Elite,' mama."

"Here we are, George, honey," she called out. "What a night!"

Winona stared up at the sky. "God, I beseech thee. I'm fourteen, God. Let a man marry me! In India they marry at *ten.*" She closed her eyes. "Rachel, lead me into that thing." She held her hand out. "Lead me. Oh God, get me out of this utterly tacky life! Will anybody help me or do I have to do it myself?"

35

A NEW FAMILY moved in on Anderson Street, down one house from the corner of Maplewood. Mr. and Mrs. Hoyle and their two grown daughters, Helen and Mary, weren't like people in town, they were Catholics. Unusual. The Catholic church was over the other side of the C. M., ST. P., & P. tracks and every Sunday before breakfast, dowdy Mr. and Mrs. Hoyle and their two stylish daughters set off on the walk across the tracks past the Winona Tool and Gear Company to St. Malachy's.

Helen worked in Minneapolis and came home for weekends. Mary Hoyle taught third grade in the West Winona grammar school. Every morning, looking dashing, she walked the mile and a half to West Winona. She not only looked dashing, but something else. Was it what Mrs. Brigham called common? Was it what Beryl called tough? Was it anything to do with being Catholic? Winona admired it and the Hoyle girls. They suggested fellows and the rustle of silk, a life beyond Anderson Street they didn't tell their dowdy mother and father about, but confessed on Sunday to the priest out of sight in the box. Was it tough? Was it common? Was it wicked? Was it all three? Whatever it was, acquire it. She told Beryl she was going to Anna's and set off for West Winona. By Garvin Heights quarry she hovered near the school gate, eye out for Mary Hoyle. She'd act as though she just happened to be walking there. Why be devious? Was it one more secret? And why not one more? Was life more exciting with secrets? If she was a Catholic would she tell the priest about Mr. Holbrook? Maybe tell Mary about the Sanburn Street altar and maybe become a Catholic. Who else wore a cross? Wearing a cross wasn't tough or common, but it *was* different. If she couldn't look Viennese like Lily Corey, could she look Catholic like Mary Hoyle? Would it say in *Green Book* magazine "Winona Lloyd, the Catholic actress who always wears a golden cross on a golden chain"? Even when she got in bed with a fellow, she would never take off her golden cross on the golden chain. Maybe someday, somebody she did it with would give her a *diamond* cross on a *diamond* chain. Wouldn't that look great? Wouldn't that be like she was awfully good in bed?

She walked back and forth along West Garvin Street, eye out for Mary, and there she came, red swagger coat open, showing her black-and-white-checked wool dress, golden cross on a golden chain.

"Hi." It was Mary Hoyle's dark voice, with an overtone of *I wouldn't tell this to everybody.*

Winona looked around as though, *Who did she know on West Garvin?*

Mary Hoyle waved. It had worked out. Mary took her arm and gave it a little squeeze. "Walking home?" she asked.

"You bet."

Off they went in step, in sympathy. Anyone but Mary Hoyle would have asked, "What are you doing way out here?" Mary Hoyle didn't. She just said, "Hi." Maybe that's what made the Hoyle girls different, they didn't ask anybody why and they didn't *tell* anybody.

"How did you happen to be walking with Mary Hoyle?" asked Beryl.

"I ran into her."

"She's so much older than you."

"Oh, she likes me."

"Didn't you tell me you were going to Anna's?"

"She was off somewhere, so I went for a stroll, ran into Mary."

"You call her Mary?"

"Oh, did I?"

She sat down at the piano, began banging the keyboard and singing:

Get out and get under
He had to get under
To fix up his little machine!

"Do you have to scream so?" asked Beryl. "Mr. Hanson's sitting out there glaring at you."

Winona stopped. Would she leave on the golden cross when Mr. Wilson looked at her breasts?

36

BERYL AND GEORGE and Winona cut peonies and snowballs from the Penniman grounds, then got into the Elite delivery truck and drove down past the Winona Tool and Gear factory to St. Matthew's Episcopal Church. Mrs. Brigham had said no decorations, but there were a lot of snowballs and peonies left after she and Joe had taken an armful out to Addie and to Charlie. George and Beryl and Winona banked the altar and filled the church vases.

Reverend Mills came in and admired the flowers. "They telephoned they're on their way."

The door opened and handsome Joe Penniman came in, his arm around Mrs. Brigham. She leaned over and kissed Winona and Beryl and George, while Mr. Penniman shook hands with Reverend Mills and came back to shake hands with the Snowdens and Winona.

"How *pretty* you made it!" said Mrs. Brigham.

Beryl held out the turquoise ring Mrs. Macchi had bought for the baby. Mrs. Brigham laughed. "Something old, that's me, something new, that's Joe, something borrowed, give me a penny, George."

He did.

"And something blue. That's this." She tucked the

turquoise ring inside her glove and kissed Winona.

"Now then, the Reverend's got souls to save," said Mr. Penniman. "Shall we?"

He held out his big hand to Mrs. Brigham. She looked at him sweetly and went with him. As she walked to the altar, the skirt of her dark blue silk suit showed a flash of pearly gray taffeta petticoat, so feminine it made her seem adorable. Mrs. Brigham from Glorieta, who didn't like Mr. Barney's sign "Garage and Implements," now going to be Mrs. Joseph Penniman and live in the big white mansion with the columns up on Johnson Avenue. Mrs. Brigham with her own Packard car and her own chauffeur, Vernon.

"Do you take this woman?"

"I do."

"Do you?"

"I do."

Mr. Penniman leaned over and kissed her, there was no more Mrs. Brigham. It was Mrs. Joseph Penniman of Johnson Avenue.

37

"Auntie cora and Auntie Belle invite you for a week to Green Isle," wrote Rachel.

Green Isle, Wisconsin, was where Auntie Cora and Auntie Belle had their summer home, and as soon as school closed the Dudley girls and Honoria joined them there. Beryl folded Winona's grammar school graduation dress into the suitcase they'd bought in Albuquerque for the journey east. Except for Beryl's wedding trip it had collected dust under the eaves. George brought it down. It was going to Green Isle.

"Rachel and Kitty's suitcase is old too," said Winona, "but Honoria has a whole trunk of her own that's shiny brown and on the side is *HD* in shiny brass tacks and inside the lid are rose-satin ribbon stripes; Mr. Hardwick gave it to her. The Auntie Cora is Mr. Hardwick's secretary so she's got lots of money. He probably lets someone else do the stenography and just cuddles Auntie Cora."

"What makes you get those ideas?"

"I'm fourteen going on fifteen. Florence Swenson's Aunt Mabel got married at fifteen and had little Mabel at sixteen. She's very rich and lives in Chicago at the

Auditorium Annex. Florence says some people now call it the Congress Hotel."

Beryl went with Winona on the train to Minneapolis, where Mr. Runnells introduced himself, then he and Winona took the train into the Wisconsin woods.

"With Mr. Runnells I'll ride in a parlor car," she told her mother and George, but the Green Junction train didn't have one. Mr. Runnells bought all the latest magazines and a box of Huyler's chocolates from New York City and a big package of presents.

At Green Junction a carriage met them for the drive to Green Isle. Auntie Cora's house was big and rambling and handsome like the Minneapolis apartment and full of expensive things. In Auntie Belle's room was a beautiful dressing table covered with silver brushes and two silver combs and a big and small silver mirror and articles for every imaginable use. No one was allowed to go into Auntie Cora's room, but one afternoon when the aunts were out for a drive, Rachel let Winona peek in. Gold mirrors and gold brushes on Auntie Cora's dressing room table.

"It's real solid gold," said Rachel, "and that crystal bottle is Attar of Roses."

"Perfumerie?" Winona was sure she was wrong.

Rachel nodded. "Don't touch it, it's very expensive."

"Hammet's sells perfumerie, but nobody likes it."

"I guess Auntie Cora does."

Mr. Runnells put up at the Islesford House but came over for lunch and dinner. The big package of presents was for everybody.

Winona wrote home, "Mr. Runnells brought us each an expensive game. I'm wild about him. Auntie Cora has real solid gold brushes, but I'm not supposed to have seen them. Probably they're from the one she's the secretary of, Mr. Hardwick. He has a family spends summers up in Crystal Lake in a mansion, so Auntie Cora has the whole summer off. I bet he misses her. She must look gorgeous brushing her gold-colored hair with gold brushes."

Mr. Runnells was the only visitor. Rachel said he came each weekend, went back to Minneapolis on the late Sunday afternoon train. After he left it was just the aunts and the Dudley girls. No one ever called or ran in. The Wesselhoeft place was across the road and the girls played with Emily Wesselhoeft and her brothers but never brought them back to Auntie Cora's.

On Sunday Auntie Belle went to church, Mr. Runnells stayed at the Islesford House till church was over, Auntie Cora stayed in her room. Sunday night came and went. The carriage pulled up to take Mr. Runnels and Winona to Green Junction. She thanked Auntie Cora and was kissed by Auntie Belle and Rachel and Honoria and Kitty. The grand days were over. But were they? They'd let her see the world where people had everything. And what did they do to get everything? Did Mr. Runnells pay for things for Auntie Belle and did Mr. Hardwick for Auntie Cora? Did Mr. Hardwick go out to the beautiful Minneapolis apartment, close the door and do things to Auntie Cora? Did Mr. Runnells have Auntie Belle come to see him? They were millionaires and she must find one. Why was fourteen going on fifteen too young? She had the curse every month. That meant she could get married and have a baby. Did Green Isle and a handsome apartment in Minneapolis happen overnight? Didn't silver bowls of hothouse daffodils on the table have to be arranged for? Let her mother settle for George and Maplewood Avenue.

Didn't Florence Swenson's Aunt Mabel run away and get married to a Chicago stockbroker at fifteen? Was Mr. Runnells a stockbroker? Mr. Wilson was. Mr. Runnells had to be a millionaire, what if she married him next year when she was fifteen and had a baby like little Mabel the year after? She looked out the corner of her eye at him reading *McClure's* magazine. If she got him to kiss her would he marry her? Next fourteenth of June she'd be fifteen, but he was Auntie Belle's. Did Mr. Runnells get in bed with Auntie Belle and do that to her so that he'd give her all the things? Did Auntie Cora let Mr. Hardwick? Did he give her that scary feeling? Did Mr. Runnells give Auntie Belle that feeling Mr. Holbrook gave her? Maybe he did it better than Mr. Holbrook. Probably it could be so great it made Mr. Runnells and Mr. Hardwick want to buy everything so their ladies would be ready when they wanted to.

38

BACK AT HOME she thought about Mr. Runnells. A girl had to get a man to get her whatever she wanted. Then when you got the man, what do you do so he keeps wanting to? Would Mr. Wilson keep wanting to? He had money, had seen her drawers, should she go all the way? And how would she find out what was all the way?

Mr. Wilson was old, but so was Mr. Holbrook. Mr. Holbrook? How long since she'd seen him? Maybe walk down Station Street.

In the door, Mr. Holbrook was talking to a customer. Winona walked past him, pretended to look at a ladder, then at a long curtain, near the back of the store where Mr. Holbrook's desk was.

"Good-bye," said Mr. Holbrook. The customer left, carrying her package.

"You neglected me." He sat down at his desk, drew her onto his lap. Still that scary feeling. He reached under her skirt. She stopped his hand. But it couldn't be stopped.

"Oh." His hand had touched the napkin. His mouth covered hers, his hand stayed where it was. "You're a big girl. No more maple sugar, no more daisies." He laughed.

"You want to come down to my cottage on the river?"
His mouth covered hers, his hand reached under her
white cotton shirtwaist, teased the nipple, already stiff.
"You're a big girl, come down when you stop." He undid
two buttons of her shirtwaist and kissed each pink nipple. "You like it?"

"Maybe." She slid off his lap and went. Maybe she'd
go. Maybe Mr. Holbrook would show her what Beryl
and George did when they closed the door. What Auntie
Cora and Auntie Belle did to get everything expensive.

She walked up to Sanburn Street where she'd been a
little girl with a secret. Was growing older always full of
secrets? Why couldn't she ask her mother things? When
she was little in Glorieta she could tell her anything, and
ask her too. Now things didn't get talked about. Did it
start with that first time at Mr. Holbrook's when he gave
her the maple sugar? Then she saw her mother and Mrs.
Brigham looking in the store window and was going to
pretend she didn't see them. She went with them but
didn't tell. Why had she told about Mr. Barney and Nita
Macchi? Was that because it was scary but she didn't
like it? With Mr. Holbrook it was scary but she liked it.
If you like it, then does that make it a secret? Is that why
her mother never talked about George and the closed
door?

39

AN ACTRESS was coming to town. Mike Dineen flicked a whisk broom over his horse's back and across the seat of his hack.

"Hi, George," he called. "Show people are on the train."

Winona jumped out of the jitney and George gave his hand to Beryl.

"Mama, if the train's late, I'm going to kill myself."

George looked up the track. "Why would it be?"

"Because I want it to be on time. If you want a thing terribly, it takes longer than if you just sort of want it."

"Where'd you get that?" asked George, half dubious, half impressed.

"It's my belief."

"Hiya, George." Hans Hendriksen strolled over from his bus.

"Henny."

Winona gave her mother a look of dismay. "What's he have to talk to us for?" she whispered.

"The troupe's coming in on this train." Henny looked up the track.

George nodded. "We're meeting the leading lady."

Winona's eyes shot up to the sky. "Oh God, please don't let Henny Hendriksen be talking to us when Eva Dill gets off the train."

"She's a friend of Beryl's. She's going to spend the night at our house."

"Mama, why does George have to talk it all over? Did you say her hair is light blonde?"

"How do I know? I haven't seen her since the show, I told you. Not since Baraboo, Wisconsin, when I left."

"You said Green Bay."

"I got married in Green Bay, but I had to give notice. By the time we got to Green Bay, she'd changed her hair from auburn to blonde."

"Why did you stop being an actress? Why? Tell me why. Were you pregnant and had to?"

George strolled off a little way.

"George, come back here."

"Mama, I'd be happy to be born out of wedlock."

"George." Beryl grabbed his head and kissed him full on the mouth.

"Mama, we're out here on the station platform!"

"Shut up!" Beryl's eyes were deep on George. "I haven't anything to tell that you can't hear, George."

Winona took a deep breath. "I can live through anything. I'm different and that's my strength. God gives those he loves shining armor to—"

The train rumbled way up the tracks.

Winona's face went scarlet. "Oh, beloved Jesus, here she comes! It's only swearing when you don't stick in a 'beloved'. Thank you, God, for letting me meet an actress. That's what I may have to become."

The train was slowing down.

"Hold your stomach in, mama, hold it in all day."

"They're in the back car." Beryl jumped up and down and started running.

"Where, mama?" Winona ran ahead of her. "How could you know?"

"Their suitcases all got show stickers. There she is!" An adorable golden head. "Beryl!"

"Mama, if I move, I'll faint."

"Beryl, darling." It was a luscious voice that could charm a man or a matinee. For Winona, it opened a new world. No one in Glorieta or Minnesota sounded like that.

"Eva!" Beryl started laughing.

Sapphire eyes sparkled at George. "Beryl, you picked a pip."

Beryl went the color of a June rose.

"Let me hoist that suitcase." Why did George's neck get red?

Beryl hugged Eva tight. "I feel I'm back in the show." She was still laughing.

"She's pretty sweet, huh, Georgie boy?" asked Eva.

"She's a peach and so are you."

Eva bowed.

> My mother thanks you,
> My father thanks you,
> My sister thanks you,
> And *I* thank you.

"May I have the honor?" Winona moved gracefully in front of Eva Dill. "I'm Winona."

Eva Dill chose an expression of ravished astonishment. "This *big?*"

"You're the first actress I ever met." She swept a curtsy right down to the cindery earth like Miss Burns had trained them for the finish of the rose dance.

"Where did she learn to be so graceful?"

George started down the platform.

"Eva, kid," Beryl hugged her again.

"My God," Eva hugged back.

"Miss Dill, I wish the station platform was strewn with Attar of Roses and I could present you with a real gold toilet set."

"Adorable." Eva and Beryl walked toward George. "You've got everything, kiddo. You know where I made my mistake? The night you met Jack. Maybe I should have tried to get him, but you not only got Jack, you got this hunk of bliss." She lit up her smile for George. "Oh, I *gotta* get somebody for *me!*"

Winona touched Eva's arm. "Miss Dill, don't give a darn about getting a husband. To be on the stage is more remarkable. Could you, out of your infinite goodness, show me the way how? I don't want to be on the stage just to be on the stage, it's to have people crazy about me and meet fellows and not get married. Mama wanted to, but *I* don't and don't *you,* Miss Dill, *help* me get somewhere."

My God, thought Eva Dill, it's the others who are going to need help. This one's really *something.*

40

AFTER THE SHOW George and Beryl and Winona went behind the scenes to Eva's dressing room. To George and Winona it was something different, to Beryl it was a reminder. She never wanted to go back to that life.

"Only show I ever liked being in," said Beryl, "was that one Lillian Russell was the star."

"Henpecks," said Eva.

"Weber and Fields and Lillian Russell. She was great to me."

At the house Eva and Beryl never stopped talking. George had made a chicken à la king in the chafing dish, a wedding present from the McFarland Hardware Company. Served on toast it was good. Eva and Beryl talked and ate, George was happy if Beryl was happy, and Winona listened and thought. The show was a road tour company of a New York musical comedy, *The Three Twins.* Eva sang and danced and made a hit. Her curly hair was blonde. There were four showgirls that didn't do anything but just move around, wear slinky clothes and act as though they looked great. Winona thought about them. About Eva. About going places. Eva had to meet the company at the railroad station at six o'clock in the morning. The show moved on to Albert Lea to play tomorrow night. Eva said these one-nighters were just for a while, they were on their way to the Coast and better times. A little worry because tonight the theatre wasn't full, but it was pretty good.

"It's not a show town," said Beryl, "but they liked it."

Winona thought. It looked like fun, it looked like you could be free and easy, it looked like a chance to get going. Eva could sing and dance. All the dancing *she* knew was Miss Burns's lessons and the crazy dances she did when Anna played the piano. But what about those girls that just slinked around? Not one looked as good as she would. Would Eva help her? What would her mother say? What would her mother say if she said she was going to be kept by Mr. Wilson, who her mother had never even met? Or Mr. Runnells, who she did meet? So why think of asking her mother about getting Eva to get her in a show? She was going to be fifteen next month. At Marian Brown's party when they played post office, she got four special delivery letters, which was one more than any other girl got. Special delivery letters meant step into Marian's back hall and the boy who called it out kissed her. Not like Mr. Holbrook, just a kiss, except Tacks Johnson. He was a high school senior and captain of the football team. His kiss was long.

"Aunt Eva?"

Eva Dill turned around.

"How did you know how to be an actress? Did you learn it in a school?"

"I went to the Alviene School in New York, dear, but a lot of people don't. Beryl, you never did."

"No."

"Mama, how did you know how?"

"There was a stock company in Boston, and my girl-friend and I went to see the manager and he heard me sing and said I could play a little part."

"Did those tall girls go to school, do you think?"

"The showgirls? They took lessons, I guess. They get taught to walk the way to make the most of their looks and, yuh, they studied something, but, y'know, not too much. Oh, Beryl, did I tell you my sister married Mr. Brophy, who owns Brophy's Café, in Minneapolis? She's coming to Albert Lea tomorrow night. We don't play Minneapolis."

41

WINONA LOST no time. She wrote a letter.

> Mrs. Brophy
> c/o Brophy's Café
> Minneapolis, Minn.

She used her yellow paper with *WL* engraved on it in dark red.

Dear Mrs. Brophy,

I am a friend of your sister Eva Dill. I am not only a friend, but a great admirer. I saw her last night in *The Three Twins*. Isn't she a wonder! What *I* wonder is, would you let me come to see you, I come to Minneapolis all the time and I would so like to talk to you. You see, I am going on the stage and I know how to do it, but I thought talking to you who knows how Eva did it would be a real help.

If you would write me, I live at

      41 Maplewood Avenue
      Winona, Minn.

God bless you,

Winona Lloyd

P.S. I don't suppose you'd think of telephoning, but if you wanted to, we have a telephone. 491-M.

W.L.

Three days later the phone rang and it was Mrs. Brophy. Would Winona want to come Saturday and spend the night, she could ask anybody at the Minneapolis station which trolley went past her house, 55 Red Star Street. The trolley was marked "West Lake" and ran every half hour.

"Mama, what'll I wear? I have to look *great*. It's only Thursday, could you finish my black-striped blazer? Mama, if you ever cared about me! Mama!"

"Eva told me Mr. Brophy is a toughie. It isn't a café, it's a saloon."

"Mama, I'm not an ignorant nobody. He won't ask me to fill up on liquor. I'm going to be with his *wife.* Mama, I am old enough to know how to behave. Mama, can you *really* finish my blazer?"

42

MRS. BROPHY seemed glad to see Winona. She showed her all the pictures she had of Eva and she talked and talked but didn't seem to know too much about how her sister got started, nor was she too interested. Mostly she was glad to have someone to talk to.

Just before supper Mr. Brophy arrived. He read the newspaper through supper, which they ate in the kitchen. Afterward they still sat there, though the house had a dining room. Mr. Brophy was big and beefy and never stopped reading the paper. From time to time he said, "More coffee," and turned back to the news. "Goddammit, I oughta have my saloon in Chicago, they're open to any hour." He shook his head at fate landing him in Minneapolis and spit on the floor.

The next morning Winona took the trolley into Minnie and the noon train home.

"Was it nice?"

"All right."

"Is he a toughie?"
"No, but he keeps to himself."
"Was Eva's sister a help?"
"Oh, yes."
Did Winona keep to *herself*?

43

Dear Anna,

How is it up at the lake? I just feel like writing you a letter. You know I went to Minneapolis to spend the night with Eva Dill's sister. She wanted me to stay longer, but I became unwell and thought by afternoon I would be in such an agony of pain, home would be the place for me. Eva Dill's sister, Mrs. Brophy, is adorable and I got a lot from her. Mr. Brophy keeps to himself. I did not have cramps like I usually do so Florence Crowell came over for lunch and we had an awfully good time. Between us we garnered in most of the scandal that's around. She's darling. Last night Mary Hoyle and I went for a walk and afterwards she came over. She's full of the dickens. Loads of fun. I'm more and more crazier about her, she knows a man that's a divorcé she's going to introduce me to. She says he's English and has a nifty blonde mustache. Guess what kind of car he has, a battleship gray Mercedes.

Did I tell you my coat is absolutely charming? Collar and cuffs are pequoed yellow quince chartreuse. Mama had to take it to Minnie to get it done but I had to have it. And a Byron collar of soft lawn mama embroidered in sprays of lily-of-the-valley. I may wear it in some show I *may* be going to do.

Love,

Winona

P.S. Do you like Reflection for a name? Maybe I'm going on the stage, but keep it under your hat.
    W.

44

Dear Mrs. Brophy,

Thanks for the lingerie clasps you sent for my going-away present. Even more of a present was all the talk you gave me about Eva

Dill. Tomorrow I leave for Chicago and live at her boarding house and go to Musical Comedy School. It's the thrill of a lifetime. Thank you for the lingerie clasps. I will write you from Chicago.

Yours in hysterics,

Winona

45

BERYL SAT on the edge of the black leather armchair that had belonged to George's father. "I never really thought this day would come, babe." She looked miserable. "I sure wish I could have talked you round not to go."

The parlor was quiet. Quiet.

Winona studied the room. "I'm going to memorize it. Y'know what I hate most, mama? Lampshades and doilies and how to make a light sponge cake. I don't belong home, mama, if I had to, I'd die. After Glorieta I guess this town looked fine, but—"

"Yes, it did."

"And you got George."

"What if *you* fall in love?" Beryl had tears in her blue eyes.

"I wouldn't."

"Lots of people do."

"Not me. You got George, mama, but I don't want to love anybody. That's my strength. I'm undivided, mama, I got blinders on me, I only see where I can go *somewheres.* I know I'm beautiful and I'm bright and I guess the way to get somewhere is get a fellow. I got to learn how. I knew people did something, but *what?* And I don't *know* is it fun or is it just what you have to do to get someone hooked? So I asked Larry Dineen did he want to? It was last month, right after the curse. We were walking home from Anna's party. He'd kissed me, then reached inside my yellow silk muslin to touch my breasts, and I said, 'You want to?' 'Sure, down to Butler's Pond there's a place behind some bushes.' "

Beryl buried her face in her hands.

"He took his pants off and I took my yellow silk muslin off and hung it on a bush and my chemise and my drawers. 'Lay down,' said Larry. He certainly knew. 'Spread your legs wide, so I can get in.' He hurt. He was too big for me or maybe my place is too small. Too small *yet.* It was the last day I was fourteen. I started to bleed. 'Have you got the curse?' he said, sore. 'No.' He did like George does to you when I hear the bed creak and wonder if you left your silk nightgown on or took it off so George could look. I don't know if you always knew how to do it good, but I'm goin' to learn to do it great to make me rich and get everything."

"What didn't I do that I *should* have?"

"Nothing. You settled for George and sponge cake and

113

soap that's handmade, mama, and you're the wife of the man runs the best grocery store in Winona. The only rich guy is Mr. Penniman and Mrs. Brigham got *him.* Are they too old to do it? See, I really don't know anything, mama."

George came up the piazza steps. "Time to go." He lifted her suitcase into the Pierce-Arrow. They drove down Maplewood, turned the car up Station Street, past Mr. Holbrook's hardware store, over the bridge, past the post office and down to the station platform. Larry Dineen was driving Mike's hack. Winona didn't look at him. George helped Beryl out. Winona jumped out on her own. George carried the suitcase.

"Yoo-hoo!" It was Anna to say good-bye.

Mr. and Mrs. Penniman's Packard pulled up.

George held Beryl's hand. "Give our best to Eva."

Beryl's face was flushed. "What if Eva doesn't meet you in Chicago?" Even though Winona had gotten away she still said those mother-things.

"Eva will, mama. If she doesn't, I'll get a trolley or a bus out to Mrs. Newbury's boarding house."

"Eva'll meet her." George smiled lovingly at Beryl.

Up the track a puff of white smoke, the rumble of the 2:10 for Minneapolis.

Beryl put her arms around Winona. "I wish I'd been a better mother."

Mrs. Penniman came just in time to hear. She gave Beryl a thump on the shoulder. "You're the best and I've been around since before there was this somebody who's leaving to be a somebody."

"Mama, you've been good, but I'm going to make it and mothers only give advice that doesn't let you. Good-bye, George, I guess I like you again. Anna, write what people say."

The train stopped.

George hoisted up her suitcase. Mr. Penniman tipped his hat. Mrs. Penniman had her arm around Beryl.

Anna hollered, "When you come back, you'll be famous!"

"I'll be different."

Lawrence Dineen leaned out of the hack and waved. He'd served his purpose.

George held on to Beryl and Mrs. Penniman. The three important people in her life. And Lawrence Dineen, for a while.

Mrs. Watson ran across the station platform and her husband helped her on the train. He looked approvingly at her black-and-white-checked suit with an orange satin shirtwaist. Winona followed her up the car steps. "All aboard!" called Mr. Watson and got back on.

Winona turned for a last look.

"Get along inside, Winona, the train's starting." Mr. Watson gave her a push through the door.

"Mama, good-bye." A west-bound freight train rumbled past and cut her off.

46

INSIDE THE CAR Mrs. Watson was sitting beside Mr. Drake. Mr. Watson made sure his wife and Mr. Drake were comfortable, then collected Winona's ticket. "You going on to Chicago?" he asked.

"Yes."

Mr. Watson shook his finger at her. "Be a good girl."

Why was it so great to be a good girl? Was Mr. Watson's wife a good girl? Mama had been, and where had she gotten? Mrs. Watson didn't look like a good girl, she looked like something was going on with her and Mr. Drake. Maybe Mrs. Watson would get somewhere.

Winona watched the towns rush past her. Across the aisle a man looked over the top of his newspaper and smiled. Would her mother have described him as a New York man?

Her mother said New York men were all tall with white faces and black hair slicked down like patent leather. She said they put on a silk shirt Sundays and holidays whether anyone was around or not. The man across the aisle was wearing a silk shirt and his suitcase had a sticker on it, Hotel McAlpin. Why have a scary feeling? She was leaving where doing it was scary. She

was going east where people did it with fellows who
bought them Attar of Roses and paid the bills and got
in bed with them. In Chicago, would Eva introduce her
to fellows? She had the looks, now use them.

47

EVA WAS AT the gate. She kissed Winona. "You're a beaut.
Are you *really* only fifteen?"

"But old for my age. Oh, Aunt Eva, I *want* to be here."

"Give me your trunk check." They went to the bag-
gage office. They said the trunk would be at Mrs. Newbury's this afternoon, tomorrow morning the latest.

Winona picked up her suitcase.

"We'll splurge on a taxi." Eva hailed a Parmalee cab.
"Four twenty-one North Rush."

"It's gotta be North, there *isn't* a *South,*" said the driver.

"That's right, I always forget."

Winona looked out at Chicago. It was going to start
here.

"I went down to the Chicago School of Musical Comedy," said Eva. "It looks all right, they expect you tomorrow. I told them you weren't going in for singing or
dancing, just enough to let you train for a showgirl. I said
you needed posture, learn to walk the showgirl step,

makeup, all the things that would give you a great appearance, but I didn't reckon with what you'd done. You're a real stunner! And red hair doesn't hurt, look at Billie Burke. And you have Beryl's, only isn't yours redder?"

"She and George send their love."

"You'll miss them."

"Aunt Eva, they're for there, and I'm for Chicago, and what I'm really for is New York. Aunt Eva, I *got* to *make* it!"

"You will. Beautiful, with long legs, red hair, a lot of will power and go. You'll get what you want."

Four twenty-one Rush. The taxi screeched to a stop.

Mrs. Newbury's boarding house was nothing like Mrs. Helmersen's. Mrs. Newbury had all theatre people, vaudeville, musical comedy and dramatic. She was a stout, ladylike woman with pride in her business, and saw to it that it lived up to its name. Everybody in show business knew to stop at Mrs. Newbury's in Chicago unless you were in a "high-salary class" and could go to the Congress or Blackstone.

"Just a hall bedroom," said Eva.

"Third floor, looks out on Rush," explained Mrs. Newbury. "Down the hall is the WC, next door to the bathroom. When you're wanted on the phone, Molly on our switchboard will ring three bells, then everybody on the third floor leans over the stair rail and Molly calls out the name. If it's for you, you come down to the first floor wall telephone and you're permitted to come down in your wrapper."

For the first time Winona was on her own. She had a bed, a bureau, a chair, curtain with clotheshooks behind it, a basin and running water, a window, a key. The start.

"They serve dinner five-thirty," said Eva, "then I go down to the theatre. *Little Dolly Daydreams* is a hit, Dennis Ryan, the star, is a big Chicago favorite. Want to come down with me tonight, sit in the dressing room?"

"Great!"

"My boyfriend's in the show too, Rex Cherry. He lives here, you'll meet him at dinner. We're going to get married when the run ends and we get back to New York."

At dinner Winona met Rex. He and Eva and she had a table to themselves.

Rex was good-looking, younger than Aunt Eva. Fresh. "My God!" he exclaimed. "Is this the little fifteen-year-old?"

Winona used her smile that used all of her. "Aunt Eva, you didn't say Rex was like this."

"Call me Eva, that Aunt Eva is for old folks. On stage we're all the same age."

Under the table Rex's knee touched Winona. Was it accidental? Above the table he looked deep into Eva's eyes.

48

"Winona?"

"Yes."

"It's Lily Corey."

"Mrs. Corey!" She had really called up!

"My sister wrote me to get in touch with you. Dearie, are you free tonight? It's a party. Evening clothes. Can I come and change in your room? It's going to be terribly swell. Watson Dahl, one of the Philadelphia Dahls and an Irish lord. Sound dandy?"

"My dear!" All of a sudden she was going to be friends with Mrs. Corey!

"Pretty good for two Minnesota girls, huh? They're both very sporty so wear some eye-catcher, I want the men to *adore* you. Oh, and we'll make a date for you to come out to our house in Evanston and really get acquainted. Come when Frank's on a trip. I'll be at your place about six. It'll be dinner and the whole evening. Maybe you'll come home engaged to a lord! That'll be more than going to the musical comedy school. Ta-ta!" Lily had hung up.

Did she sound fast? She didn't sound married. Winona went into the office. "Big party tonight, Molly.

I'm going out with an Irish lord."

"That'll get you buckwheats!"

"Very sporty. He's supposed to be a darb. My friend whose mother and sister live in my hometown, Mrs. Corey, is coming in around six. Let her come right up."

"What's her name?"

"Corey. Mrs. Corey. Very beautiful and terribly rich."

"Then why is she dropping in here?"

"Because she's my *friend*, I told you, she's from the place I used to live. Then she married this very rich man that owns all the milk in Illinois, they have a tremendous estate in Evanston."

"She bringing you in some milk?"

"Of course not. Lily's husband is rich and nifty, but he has some sort of asthma."

"Too much milk."

"It keeps him from enjoying his money. He doesn't go out a lot, so Lily enjoys it. She's adorable. Wait till you see her clothes! Oodles of coats, her sister says she has a crush on coats, and shoes! Her sister says she has so many even *she* doesn't know how many she has!"

"Ask her if she'd like me to come out to Evanston and count 'em. And for a small consideration, keep her husband breathing while she's laying friends in town."

Winona started up the stairs. It was a matinee day, so Eva was at the theatre. She'd leave a note where she'd gone.

Lily and Winona met the gentlemen at the Blackstone Hotel's elegant dining room. It was the first time she had been in a grand restaurant. Did grand mean stiff? The Irish lord was short on conversation and seemed preoccupied with his dinner. Lily was vivacious as a siren should be who knows she looks dazzling. Her tall, slender figure offered temptation under chiffon that winked and twinkled silver stars. It made Winona feel clumsy.

The Philadelphia society man, Mr. Dahl, didn't add to the gaiety. He didn't seem as taken with Lily as he was with liquor. Dinner over, he suggested they go to the Bull Ring, a new dance place over in the Loop.

"Smile, baby," whispered Lily. "People fall for even just nothing but a smile."

Winona smiled at the lord, who thought she had asked him something. "Beg pardon?" he asked.

"What?" asked Winona, smiling.

"I thought you said something."

"No," she smiled.

The Bull Ring was darkly lit, red tablecloths. The lord had caught Watson Dahl's interest in drink.

"Smile," whispered Lily.

Winona felt a hand on her knee. It fumbled and moved higher. "Smile," Lily had said. She was across the table.

"Isn't her shape nifty?" she asked the lord.

"Beg pardon?"

The hand stayed its course and Winona wondered what to do about it. She was wearing a dress of Beryl's that Mrs. Brigham and Beryl had made when she and George went to Kansas City to visit his mother. It was pearl-gray challis, and to make up for the material they had worked out patterns with gray velvet baby ribbon and French knots. It had a bolero, but for evening Winona wore it with her pale gray georgette blouse Beryl had made for Chicago. Winona put the skirt on ribbon suspenders and pulled it up high under her breasts to look Empire style, like the pictures in *Elite* magazine.

"Dance?" asked Watson Dahl, and the hand left her leg.

"Oh, she's the cutest dancer," shouted Lily. "What do you think of that adorable shape?"

Watson Dahl took her hand and led her out to the Bull Ring floor. She loved to dance, but tonight what was the matter? Why couldn't she stop being shy? Was it because of Lily, who came from her hometown?

Watson put his arms around her and they foxtrotted off. "You're a beaut," he said. "Do you always hang around with Lily?"

"Heavens, no. She's married, of course, and lives in Evanston."

"When I come in from Philadelphia, where do I call you?"

"Well, I live on Rush Street."

"Apartment?"

"No, it's Mrs. Newbury's Boarding House. My mother's friend is an actress, and I stay there with her. My mother doesn't think a young girl should live alone in the city."

"I bet you *are* a young girl." He gave her a little squeeze. "Are you?" His hand, still in hers, reached down and felt her breast.

Was Lily watching? She was so startled she snatched her hand away. The ribbon that held her skirt snapped. One side stayed Empire, the other dropped four inches, touched the floor. "Excuse me," said Winona, and fled.

She started for the ladies' room, then kept going. She

would explain to Lily. Out on the street she hailed a taxi, gave him the Rush Street address. As she raced up the steps, Mrs. Hall and Edna Hall, who shared the second floor front, were at the door getting their key out. Edna was the ingenue in *Love, Love, Love.* Mrs. Hall looked at Winona's skirt. "What did you do to your dress?"

Edna winked. "Somebody try to get in there?"

"Don't be dirty, Edna." Mrs. Hall turned to Winona. "Edna gets her clothes torn off every time I don't go out with her. You give me that tomorrow, I'll sew it up. Aren't men filthy?"

49

HAD IT BEEN a week when Rex made the date with Winona? To Eva he made excuses where he'd be that afternoon and had Winona up to a pay-in-advance room at the old Virginia Hotel. He knew how to do everything, did it, laughed when she wasn't sure. Told her, then told her she was great and made a date for next afternoon.

The musical comedy school was over at one; then the Virginia Hotel. Was Eva suspicious? She talked to the stage manager about Winona being hired as a standby.

Stage manager Coglan had given Winona a wet kiss

and a feel back of an old piece of scenery and suggested she stand by for the showgirls who claimed to have menstrual periods twice a month.

The show was at Cohan's Grand Theatre, as big a hit as in New York. Dennis Ryan, the star, was thirty-one years old, adorable, great looking, terrific actor, singer, dancer. Went on the stage when he was a child, in Gus Edwards's School Days act where he wore spectacles, played Little Johnny Boston Beans, sang and danced. His good looks stuck to him through and after adolescence. His first girl was when he was thirteen. She was older than his mother, a showgirl in *Sinbad the Sailor,* starring Eddie Foy and the Seven Little Foys. When a young Foy was sick, Dennis went on for him. One scene Eddie Foy leaned over the shiprail and threw a cake of soap to a Foy fallen overboard. "Wash yourself ashore," called Eddie. Dennis thought that was funny.

In bed one night with Winona he told her about it. She laughed, his mouth closed over her laughter. After he let go of her he lay back on the pillow. "You're only sixteen," he said, "and I'm not the first."

She shook her red curls.

"Rex?"

She shook her curls.

Dennis's hand petted the other red curls.

Winona watched him. "That was first. Mr. Holbrook put his hand under my drawers mama had made. It scared me and I loved it."

Dennis kissed her. "How old were you?"

"I was six."

"Did you go back for more?"

"Of course."

"Did Mr.—what was his name?"

"Mr. Holbrook."

"Did he ever see red curls?"

"Uh-huh."

"When did it really happen?"

"Summer before I came to Chicago to stay with Eva and go to school. When it really happened, I didn't love it, it just scared me, but I knew I had to start so I'd find out how to do it right."

Dennis pulled her closer. "Take a lesson."

He was so sure. So strong, so gentle, so unhurried, then came the minute, then nothing mattered. It was *It.*

Dennis had had every girl in the show. Eva? Probably not Eva. Probably Eva was too old. The showgirls, the ponies as they called them, were there any holdouts? Why would there be? And at the stage door there'd be long black limousines. Some society lady in his dressing room, then they'd leave together. Some young society, some older. They had homes on Lake Shore Drive, houses or apartments. Or back from the lake on the Gold Coast. Dennis could have anybody, no surprise that he would have her, the surprise was he went on having her.

Backstage he'd never paid attention to her, how did it take place? She'd gone out after the show with one of the ponies who was being kept by rich, rich Monty Behn at his French chateau model house on the Gold Coast. Pansy Corrigan had said for Winona to come up to Monty's, he had a friend from New York and needed a girl. Pansy rang the doorbell, the butler opened the door, "Mr. Behn has gone to bed, his friend left early."

"Should we flip a nickel?" Winona asked.

Pansy laughed. "I was worried about competition

even with a friend there to show you around the guest room, but with no friend, 'some other time' like they say in the funny papers. Will you be all right?"

"It's only four blocks to Mrs. Newbury's."

Pansy went in the French chateau and Winona started down Lake Shore Drive. A faint powder of snow? Take a bus. Then, coming toward her, was a great-shaped-overcoat, a derby hat.

"Hello, what are you doing out by yourself?" The overcoat and derby became Dennis Ryan. What had happened? He certainly wasn't out for a stroll, he hadn't had time to go to bed with one of the Lake Shore Drive beauties, what had happened?

Winona smiled up at him. "I was out on a date with Pansy and her fella and his friend, but I just knew I wouldn't like the friend and let Pansy down. Do you ever do that?"

"I do if I know there's someone better coming toward me in the snow." He took her arm, motioned to a taxi that had slowed down for a pickup. "College Inn please you?" he asked Winona.

"I'll love it."

Dennis opened the taxi door, Winona got in. "My girl will love the College Inn," Dennis told the driver. "There's a fiver in it if you make it by midnight."

"It's five past."

"That's just a line from a show."

The taxi raced along to Randolph Street, turned right, and all at once the Sherman House doorman was opening the door. "College Inn. Oh, good evening, Mr. Ryan."

Dennis handed out Winona.

She smiled at him. "It must be great to have everybody know you."

"This is where I live when I play Chicago."

The College Inn had a stage made of ice at one end. Charlotte, the skater from Berlin, was the first in the United States to dance on skates. On each table was a lighthouse that cast a small light, but enough. Dennis ordered chicken à la king and Veuve Clicquot. "Shall we?" He stood up and held out his arms. Great she had worn her red velvet with the slit skirt and the bodice cut low in front with the pale blue broadcloth bertha, the same color as little Honoria Dudley's Sunday school coat Mrs. Brigham said Mr. Dudley must feel bad about. Good she had gone to Miss Burns' dancing school, good Miss Burns knew about sex. Miss Burns never mentioned it at dancing school, but look at Miss Burns move and you knew she wasn't just dancing, she was making people look at her and like it. In the red velvet Winona knew the tables were looking at her. So was Dennis. He was, also, liking it.

At the table the waiter was putting out the flames under the chafing dish. Dennis, still holding Winona's hand, led her off the floor.

"All right to serve, Mr. Ryan?"

"All right, Ferdie." He gave Winona's hand a squeeze. "Why didn't we ever do this before?"

Winona gave him her smile. Did she learn that from Lily or did she know that by herself?

"You know who's crazy about you? Rex."

"Oh, no, he's Aunt Eva's. I mean, Eva's."

"Good."

Supper didn't take long. "Shall we duck out before

Charlotte? She starts in three minutes."

She nodded.

Dennis signaled Ferdie. "Sign for me and add fifteen percent."

They were in the elevator, key out, door opened into his grand suite, she was in his arms. His mouth held hers, let go, went again. "You let down Monty Behn's friend, so shouldn't this adorable dress come off and try *me?*"

The hooks and eyes separated as though they wanted to. She was in his arms with nothing between her and his elegantly tailored suit but her silk stockings and pink lace garter belt Anna Whitman had made for her going-away-to-Chicago present.

It was after three when Dennis kissed her outside Mrs. Newbury's. "Another lesson tomorrow night?"

Winona laughed. "Thank you."

"No matinee today, should *we* have one? Four o'clock, the door will be unlocked." He kissed her so gently it was like a remembered kiss. "Four o'clock."

"Four o'clock."

He was back in the taxi, she was in Mrs. Newbury's hall. It was quiet like the world stopped. Had hers begun?

50

THE COMPANY knew it. Dennis and Winona. What did Eva Dill think? Had she had worries about Rex? Afternoons missing and no convincing excuses. Should she write Beryl about Winona? Should she stay out of it?

Dennis took Winona shopping. A lovely rose wool coat lined with soft gray squirrel fur with fur sleeves, fur collar, new dresses from the grand shop on Michigan Avenue next to the Congress Hotel.

Saturday night at the Bal Tabarin in the Sherman House ballroom on the top floor, Dennis led Winona down the flight of gold stairs, her red hair tucked under a silver lace Dutch cap like Mrs. Vernon Castle had made all the rage; her lovely body in a soft silvery dress that covered everything and concealed nothing. Everybody knew Dennis Ryan and the sixteen-year-old were sleeping together.

Spring had come, they lay on the sheet, no covers.
"Do you think you'll like being Mrs. Dennis Ryan?"
Winona sat up, startled. Why had she never thought of that? Everybody knew Dennis could get any girl. Everybody knew he had stopped trying, but

did anybody think of anything more?

"Would you like that?" Dennis kissed her nearest breast. "How many before? The old man that began it and the boy to show you what it was, anyone else but Rex?"

"How did you know?"

"He likes to do it and he likes to talk about it."

"Nobody else."

"What if that night you went out with Pansy to Monty Behn's and liked his friend?"

She snuggled into his arms. "Mrs. Dennis Ryan?"

"Mr. and Mrs. Dennis Ryan."

51

DENNIS AND WINONA walked over to Spaulding's, Michigan Boulevard's elegant jewelry store. There was a stir of excitement when handsome Dennis Ryan walked in with the red-haired beauty that had caused all the talk.

"Where are the wedding rings?"

52

THE MAYOR of Chicago was going to marry them. Eva reminded Winona to send a telegram to Beryl and George. Had she known about Winona and Rex? Were they still going to get married when the show closed and they went to New York?

Chicago's mayor married them before the Wednesday matinee. After the matinee they went up to Dennis's suite.

"Take a lesson, Mrs. Ryan."

53

THE SHOW closed.

New York, the Hotel Algonquin.

How did it happen? Winona was pregnant. Had it

happened on the Twentieth Century coming to New York from Chicago? She and Dennis were still drinking Chicago rye and ginger ale, he must have been careless. Anyway, she was pregnant.

"Don't worry," said Dennis. "There's a pill you take, darling, it'll bring you around. Ergot, it's called."

How did that name roll off Dennis's tongue so fast? Had he gotten other girls pregnant? How did he get the idea so quick?

"Everybody has abortions, they're nothing! If the pill doesn't do it, I'll find a doctor. They charge a lot, but they do it. You feel punk for a day, then you're fine, except *I* won't be fine, because I'll have to lay off you for a week." He reached under her dress. "Let's do it like it's the first night we'd been walking in the snow."

So good-looking, so sexy-looking, so as though he *had* to have you, an adorable guy who knew all the everythings and that included Ergot pills, hot Epsom salt baths that *maybe*. People knew doctors that *would*. Staying at the Algonquin they could go dancing, go to shows, buy clothes. Dennis was a star who made money and also knew how to make money make *more*. He was crazy about business. His brokers were Logan and Bryan, and some mornings he would kiss the freckles on Winona's bottom, go round the corner to Logan and Bryan's Fifth Avenue office before the stock market opened.

For the Ergot pills they needed a prescription. Dennis knew someone at the Lambs Club down Forty-fourth Street whose brother was a doctor, and if Dennis gave him a signed photo he would deliver the Ergot. Six would be enough.

Winona swallowed one. "Bitter!" she said. "Oh, God! It's bitter."

What was really bitter, she took the six, they didn't work.

Nothing worked. It was going to have to be an abortion. Dennis would find a doctor. There were good ones. Meanwhile it was lovely in bed. No need to be careful. *She* was delicious, *he* was. She knew now why people closed their doors and didn't care what happened outside.

At the Lambs Club Dennis inquired. His friend whose brother the doctor had helped with the Ergot pills said his brother could go no further. Too bad, because he'd like to help, but the penalty was too steep.

Dennis asked here and there, then went to Frank Wadsworth, who had been stage carpenter for *Little Dolly Daydreams.*

54

FRANK KNEW a doctor. He was up in The Bronx and had a good reputation. Frank had never had reason to use him, but he knew others. Should he call him up? Give no names or anything, just inquire?

Dennis was grateful.

Frank called back. " 'A friend of mine,' I said, 'he's married, but don't want children.' Could he oblige? It would be fifty dollars and he could."

"Make the date," said Dennis. "Any time will be convenient."

Frank called back. "He will but he wants to talk to you. I didn't say your name, I said you're a friend, David Robbins. Same initials, but let's hope he doesn't recognize you. Probably won't, lives up in The Bronx. Probably doesn't come down to shows. He'll see you four o'clock tomorrow."

That night at the Algonquin, Winona was in his arms. She loved it, he loved it, they lay back, relaxed, warm, quivering, satisfied. Then he turned her over.

"It hurts like this."

"It won't."

"Ow!"

"Try, darling."

"No."

"I want every part of you."

"It hurts." She cried a little.

"Let me make up for it." She forgot the hurt. They went to sleep. Slept till noon. Woke and she came close to him. He didn't need urging.

Breakfast over, he dressed, took off for The Bronx.

Doctor's office was a walk-in off the street, in an old, grimy, gray stone building. Dr. Oldham's door was open from the waiting room to his office, no patients in the waiting room.

"I'm Mr. Robbins," said Dennis. "Frank Wadsworth spoke to you about me."

"Yes, I told him I would not be able to oblige his friend."

"Oh, I thought—"

"I told him he was asking an impossible service. It's against the law."

"Oh."

"I won't charge you for this visit. Good day."

Dennis went out. That night he called up Frank.

"Know all about it. He knew you. Saw you in *Ladies Day*. Turns out you're his wife's favorite. He said he wouldn't take a chance with anybody celebrated, he did say a nurse who worked part-time does it, but to don't say he said so, she's Bryant one-nine-eight-three, and to make the arrangements and for Mrs. to go alone. She might not do it if she saw *you*."

The appointment was made. Two o'clock tomorrow afternoon. She would do it. Had done it many times. She would do it in a doctor's office she borrowed. He was out of town. It was in the Lincoln Arcade at Sixty-fifth and Broadway, first floor.

"Darling, she won't do it if I'm with you."

"I'll go alone."

He put her in a taxi and got in. "I'll get out at Sixty-fourth, then I'll come back here, wait for you. Here's a hundred dollars. It won't be this much, but just in case. Oh, darling!"

The cab stopped at Sixty-fourth Street. He got out, she went on to the Lincoln Arcade, a rambling, obsolete-looking building, windows with doctors' signs, signs for a fortune-teller, sign for cornet lessons. She found the doctor's name she was looking for, rang the bell. The door was opened by an unpromising-looking bulky woman in a crumpled nurse's uniform. "Hello," she said, "I'm expectin' you."

"Yes," said Winona.

"Ever had this done to you?"

"No, I haven't."

"Well, I warn you, it's painful, but you have to put up with it and I'll be as easy as I can. Even easy it'll hurt, but you just remember the fun you had getting yourself in the family way. Did you bring the fifty dollars?"

Winona handed it to her. She tucked it into the top of her stocking.

"Follow me." She led Winona into the doctor's office. There was a big armchair. "You sit here. Oh, get your drawers off. You wear a garter belt?"

Winona nodded.

"Get that off." Roll your stocking down. You can keep your shoes on." She heated up something on a Blue Flame stove like Mrs. Holbrook's painting in Mr. Holbrook's hardware store window. She got out some shiny metal things. Winona decided better not look.

The nurse got two low stools. "Now, girlie, put each foot up on these. I gotta get a good look, so spread your legs wide. I know you know how to do that, but this time for me to get a good look, spread wider than you think you can."

Winona did. It hadn't even begun, but it was the worst day of her life. What if she said no and went back to the Algonquin? She'd have a baby. She wouldn't want a baby. Did Dennis? Probably not.

"Now hold steady. I'm going to open you up. This'll hurt, but hold steady."

She put something metal between Winona's legs.

Winona felt the metal thing stretching, stretching. She grabbed the arm of the chair.

"If you can relax, it won't hurt so."

The pain got worse. She gave a moan.

"Act like a baby and I can't do it. You have to help or I won't get in there. If you cry now, what'll you do when I get in and have to scrape your womb out?"

It was over. It was awful.

"I'll get you a cab, there's a line down the block."

Winona wondered if she could walk.

"Hold my arm. You hurt, but you're fine. I wanted to make sure. Y'know sometimes they don't do a thorough job and it's all to do over. And tell your hubby to have no sexual intercourse with you for a week. Two is safer. And for the future, the time you get caught is before and after the curse. If you don't want kids you gotta be careful. It's better if you can get him not to come inside ya. Most men don't go for that."

Dennis was at the door of the hotel. He put his arm around her, the elevator, the tenth floor. She lay down on the bed.

"Oh, darling."

"It was awful."

"Oh, darling." He got her dress off, her nightgown on.

"I'm bleeding so."

"I'm going to call Dr. James. *Now* it's all right. He can look after you."

Dr. James came. He didn't have to be told. He made an examination, handled her gently, used some ointment, said he'd be back first thing tomorrow and gave Dennis his home telephone number in case. "I'm sure she's all right, but it's hell to go through."

For two days Dr. James came to see how she was doing. She must stay in bed for two days more. Dennis looked at her with guilty eyes. "It's damn unfair, *you* get hurt and not me."

"Damn unfair *anybody* has to."

Dr. James said it had been a bungled job, but she had responded to treatment and no danger of infection.

A loving, penitent kiss and Dennis left for his meeting with Charles Dillingham to hear the music for the new Jerome Kern show Dillingham wanted to star him in.

On the table by the bed were *Theatre* magazine, *Red Book, Green Book,* but she didn't feel like reading. What if this happened *again?* And why wouldn't it? And why hadn't she even thought it would? What if it had happened after Larry Dineen? Would she have had to have a baby? Certainly nobody in Winona would do an abortion. Would anybody even know about one? Would anybody do one in Minneapolis? And how would she know who? Would Mr. Wilson know? How would he? People like him only knew about getting married and a baby was what would be expected.

Would her mother have known what to do? She'd been on the stage and certainly knew about it, would she have said Larry had to marry her?

Things went so easy, then this. Would what went on back of closed doors with her mother and George be safe now, because of that miscarriage? How did Eva Dill manage? Thoughts went back to Auntie Cora and Auntie Belle, to Lily. Lily Corey had no children. Did that just happen or did she and Mr. Corey know what to do? Or did Lily have to have abortions? Abortions! People had more than one? Who could stand it? Suddenly she was crying.

55

TWO WEEKS of not going out. Tonight dinner at Delmonico's, then the new hit, *Parlor, Bedroom and Bath.*

The doors of the Eltinge Theatre swung open and applause struck the street. Stylishly dressed men and women came out. Coming out with them were Winona and Dennis, talking excitedly. It had been a great evening.

"Hiya, sweetheart." It was Al Woods, owner of the theatre, producer of the show. His chair was tipped back against the theatre he owned. "Hello, Denny."

"What a great show!"

Al tipped his Panama back, held out his arms to Winona. "Wanna sit on my knee, sweetheart?"

She laughed. "Right on Forty-second Street?"

"You got a good shape, sweetheart. He appreciate you?" He pointed his cigar at Dennis.

"No!"

"I do," protested Dennis.

"When do I get you in a show, boy?"

"When you ask me!"

"Isn't he full of bull?" He winked at Winona. "What kind of show will you do? Up in my office is a mess of scripts. Send you one first thing tomorrow while you're still in bed. Y'ever want to change, Winona, call me up. Hey, Marty," he shouted to his business manager. "I'm going on the *Mauretania* tomorrow. Meet me home ten o'clock with the tickets. Y'wanna come along, Winona? No ticket for you, Denny, they only got one left for Winona."

56

THE SCRIPT from Al wasn't what Dennis was going to do. Nor was the new Jerome Kern show. Dennis was going to do a show without music. When he was a child actor, he'd been in straight plays, but at sixteen he went into musicals. His first he played a jockey in one starring Fritzi Scheff. Then always musicals, but now the great Belasco had sent for him to co-star in a straight comedy, *My Lulu Belle*. Lenore Ulric and he would have to black up. In a musical or a revue, Bert Williams was a big star, but in straight plays if the part called for someone black an actor blacked up.

"But what will *you* do, darling? No showgirls, no anything for *you*. Will you mind being home nights or backstage in my dressing room, then after, we'll go out stepping and make up for earlier evening? And, sweetie, money will pour in, anything you want. I have everything *I* want." He put his hand on her, kissed her. "Let's go out and celebrate. A Lucile dress. No, two Luciles and the great thing will be me taking them off. Before we go, you want to?" Clothes came off. "I never get used to you." It was perfect. Even better than perfect, all the money and excitement.

They lay there. "Let's make it three dresses. All the more to take off."

But what *would* she do with Dennis on stage and only glimpses of him if she stayed in his dressing room? What a lot of things hadn't been thought of. Never a thought about what to do alone until she was going to be alone.

The phone rang. "It's Lily. I'm in New York for a flutter!"

"Great! Did you know I'm Mrs. Dennis Ryan?"

"Of course, it was in the papers. Frank had to go off on a business trip, I'm here for a week at the Biltmore. Two Minnesota beautiful hotsie-totsies wind up in style a few blocks from the Great White Way and married to guys with lots of money."

"Do you still go back to see your family?"

"Oh, sure. My stiff-looking sister told me she'd been having an affair with someone classy there. A doctor! Don't try to guess, that's all I'll say. You never told me *you* were going to marry that adorable Dennis Ryan. First I heard, I read it in the *Chicago Tribune.* No wonder he was crazy about you, men fall for red hair. Did you love being a bride?" Lily didn't think she was alive unless she was talking.

"Dennis is at David Belasco's office. He's going to co-star with Lenore Ulric."

"Talk about sexy! Think you can hold him? Imagine Minnesota girls talking like this! Want to have lunch up at the Cascades on top of the Biltmore? We'll create a stir. Every man there will wish he could ditch the cutie he's buying lunch for and want to play footsie with you and me. See you one o'clock. Biltmore Cascades. Top floor."

Winona got into her brand-new black taffeta Boué Soeurs. Full skirt, tight waist, lowish neck with a sort of cape collar of ecru linen embroidery edged with coarse handmade ecru lace. Sleeves halfway from elbow to wrist edged with bachelor-button blue like Mrs. Brigham had planted under the dining room windows at 41 Maplewood.

With the black taffeta she wore a tucked black taffeta hat that framed her face. A wisp of hair protruded over each cheek.

She told Miss Bush on the switchboard if Mr. Ryan called, say she was having lunch with her friend Mrs. Corey from Chicago at the Biltmore Cascades.

"Mrs. Corey is at her table." The maître d' led Winona to the top beauty in the room. Lily in black chiffon, pearls, black satin tight-fitting hat, like Winona's, but with a black bird of paradise plume falling over one shoulder that added to that Viennese look. They kissed and Winona took the chair across from her. Lily had been right, every man in the room with cuties or wives would rather have been with Lily and Winona.

"You aren't going to get pregnant, are you?"

"I hope not." Winona hadn't expected to get right into it.

"Not with your shape! My God, simply *don't* let him do it. By the way, I bet you do it great. Do you?"

A right-into-things conversation.

"You never get pregnant?"

"Frank is a wonderful feller, a good provider, but not wild for sex. Know what I mean? He's not really *good* at it and knows it and doesn't feel he has to compete. He gives me everything I want, money, anything, so he figures that makes it even. By the way, make your husband beg for it. Don't be ready. It's better if you can hold him off to not more than three times a week."

The waiter offered a cold salmon on a platter. "Our specialty today."

"Looks great. Sauce verte?" To Winona, "Green sauce. They have it at the Blackstone Hotel where we went. Remember?"

"I do. I'll have it too."

"Ice coffee," said Lily.

"Me, too."

"Mrs. Corey." A handsome older man came up to the table.

"My God! Senator Putnam. How great! Winona, this is Senator Putnam, of Illinois. This is Mrs. Dennis Ryan. We're from the same hometown."

He sang, " 'Are there any more at home like you?' " To Winona, "You're too young to have seen that show, *Floradora.*"

"Me too. I'm staying here at the hotel. Frank couldn't come, so I'm here on a flutter."

"I'll call you. Would you like to dine?"

"Of course."

"I'll call." He bowed to Winona and went.

"My dear," said Lily, "want to hear a secret? He and I have a date for tonight but he didn't expect to run into me here and he doesn't want you to know it. Talk about being a politician! Talk about Foxy Grampa!"

So she was right, Lily *was* fast. She was right and she knew she was when she told Anna. Fast people are a breed apart, if you're fast yourself, you can pick one.

"What would Mr. Corey think?"

"Call him Frank. He has asthma and what he doesn't know doesn't worry him." They both laughed. "I forget how long you and Dennis? Two months?"

"Not quite."

"So you haven't cheated on him?"

Winona shook her head.

"Or he on you?"

"Of course not."

"Why 'of course'?"

"He's wild about me."

"Look out for Lenore Ulric. They say she's Belasco's girl, but there's always that

> When the boy says "will you?"
> And the girl says "Yes."

Lily's throaty voice made everything sensuous. "Never trust what a man's doing out of your sight. That's why I say, 'hold out on him.' Even if you haven't got a date with a senator, let him think you could have. And also, what else is there to do when he's playing those Wednesday and Saturday matinees?"

It was the swish of Mrs. Corey's skirt that had first made Winona tell Anna that Mrs. Corey was fast.

57

DENNIS TOOK Winona to the Ziegfeld Frolic, the most gala nightclub ever. Mr. Mortimer Burrage introduced himself to Dennis. A great admirer of his in *Little Dolly Daydreams* when it played in New York.

Dennis introduced Winona. Was Winona why Mortimer Burrage had introduced himself to Dennis?

After the Frolic, Mortimer Burrage had a table at Harry Richman's Wigwam. Will Dennis and Mrs. Ryan join his party? Winona squeezed the arm of Dennis's dinner jacket. They will. They'll meet there at the table.

Next day but one Mortimer Burrage called Mrs. Ryan at the Algonquin. Would she come to lunch at one? His apartment was over the Capitol Theatre, which he owned. Why didn't he ask Dennis? Did he know Dennis was in rehearsal?

Lunch was served, then Mortimer Burrage told the butler he didn't want to be disturbed. The butler bowed, the door closed. Mortimer Burrage opened the front of Winona's dress. Beneath it was a Boué Soeurs camisole, lace, embroidery, one flat pink chiffon rose with a deeper rose color center. Morty lifted up the rose and looked under. There was Winona's breast with the rosy nipple standing out.

"Waiting to be kissed," he said, and did.

He was seventy maybe, gray-haired, handsome, elegant, rich, a power.

His hand went under her skirt, the Boué Soeurs drawers were wide, meant for a hand, meant for Winona to lie back on the velvet brocade couch. Mortimer Burrage unbuttoned his fly and she felt something warm and soft finding its way.

"Help me," he whispered.

She was Mrs. Ryan, could she be Mrs. Burrage? What if she wasn't Mrs. B? He could do everything for her, he knew everyone. He must have been great, now he only loved it, wanted it, had to be helped. Once was all for now. He kissed her, got straightened out for his next appointment. His office was on the same floor. Wouldn't she like to let him do things for her? There was a chance in the musical at the Princess, which he had backed. Would her husband let her take a part in a show where he wasn't appearing?

At the Princess, William Randolph Hearst had his Marion Davies in the musical. There were six girls who were the beauties of the town, Marion Davies, Justine Johnstone, Patricia Ramsey, who was leaving to marry Sir Willie Wiseman. Perhaps Mortimer Burrage could put Winona in Patricia's place?

Would Dennis make it easy for Mortimer Burrage to put himself in his wife's place?

Winona was a hit. Dresses by Lucile showed off

Winona's red hair, long legs, style. Was it hers or had she picked it up at the Ziegfeld Musical Comedy School in Chicago? Wherever she acquired it, it was now Winona's. She knew she was a beauty, she knew red hair made a man want to look at it. From the Chicago Musical College she'd learned how to walk, how to use her body on stage, and from Mr. Holbrook had learned to love being handled. From Larry Dineen she'd learned what a boy did.

Eva's boyfriend Rex had skill and Dennis had shown her how to use everything she had, plus everything she'd found out, had made her quiver and be ready when *he* was ready. He was adorable, was he a sidetrack to the big way? And what would she do those long evenings when he was in the show?

58

AFTER THE divorce, Mortimer bought her Du Pont bonds, put them in an account at E. F. Hutton, bought her Standard Oil of New York. Every week there arrived three purple orchids made into a corsage, an envelope with five hundred dollars in cash attached. Every week at the Princess, she was handed her salary in an envelope. Sometimes from Morty there came something extra to go for dresses, something extra to go to Boué Soeurs for their indecent flesh-colored chiffon drawers, their chiffon nightgowns.

In her closets at the Hotel Claridge were adorable coats, an evening cape, adorable dresses, wrappers with ostrich-feather edging. Mortimer spent.

A small, claret-colored limousine was hers, *WL* on the door. Barnes, in claret-colored livery, to drive the car was gray-haired, maybe five years older than Mortimer. Mortimer Burrage knew when and where people proved trustworthy. Among those who needed watching were seventeen-year-old girls and young chauffeurs. Was he safe with Barnes? Unless he had judged wrong, Barnes was more apt to go to work on Mortimer than Winona. Barnes was an old auntie.

Mortimer Burrage had gotten her started. In the Princess show she was given a lot of publicity and getting known. She missed Dennis, she was seventeen, Mortimer Burrage was seventy. He was sweet and generous, but he was still seventy. It was all right, then sometimes it wasn't.

He was moving out to his Tarrytown house for the summer. Weekday mornings he drove to New York. Winona drove out with him sometimes after a performance of *Oh, Boy!* The bedroom next to his was fitted up in orchid taffeta and chiffon drapes. Bedcover to match, the same for the dressing table. Lovely room, and all Winona's.

The Burrage Tarrytown estate was adjacent to the Rockefellers'. Not as big, but grand and stately. His staff ran it in style. Black butler, footman, two chambermaids, chef, kitchen page. His breakfast was served in the sun parlor overlooking the Hudson River. Eight-thirty promptly. Up in his big four-poster bed Winona slept on. When she rang down, breakfast would be served in *her* room.

That was Morty's orders, but of course, nothing fools servants.

59

A WESTERN Union boy delivered the telegram. He wanted to see Winona Lloyd and told the Hotel Claridge bellboy to let him go up to her suite and he'd give him the tip.

YOUR MOTHER HAD HEART ATTACK COME FAST

GEORGE

Winona showed it to Morty. "I have to go."
"Yes."
"Can you tell them at the theatre?"
"Of course." He picked up the phone. "Columbus four-nine-six-eight." He turned to Winona. "The office will get you on the first train out of Chicago for Minneapolis. Can you be ready to go on the Century tonight? You must be at Grand Central at 5:45."
"Yes." She started to put things in her suitcase. What

things? How long would she be gone? How could this happen? How old was her mother? Her mother had only been twenty when she'd had her. Next birthday she'd be eighteen, a heart attack at thirty-eight? Pack one bag with her clothes, one bag with makeup, what else? "Oh, Morty," she burst into tears.

"Be brave, darling." He turned back to the phone, gave instructions to his office, to Miss Mitchell his long-time secretary. "Come to the hotel, Miss Mitchell, and go to the Century with her. See that she's met in Chicago."

One knew Miss Mitchell would do everything right. He hung up the receiver. "Darling, I shall miss you. I shall wait for your telegrams. I need you back."

Miss Mitchell was announced. The bellboy came up. Morty and Winona went down. He kissed her, she and Miss Mitchell went off in her claret-colored limousine, Barnes at the wheel, she was going back to Maplewood Avenue. How long was it since she had left? Today was Monday.

Miss Mitchell said the Twentieth Century would be at Chicago's La Salle Street Station tomorrow morning in time for her to take the Minneapolis St. Paul and Union Pacific. She would get to Minneapolis Wednesday. Then the train to Winona. Mr. Burrage's office would let her mother's husband, Mr. George Snowden, know what train to meet. Mr. Burrage's associate in Chicago would be at the La Salle Street Station to put her on the train to Minneapolis.

Winona was trying to remember.

Miss Mitchell had it all typed out. "It's a long journey."

Time to think, time to weep, time to wonder. Miss Mitchell gave the porter *Vogue, Vanity Fair, Judge, Smart Set, Theatre Magazine* to put in Winona's drawing room. Also a sizable tip.

In Chicago Mr. Asa Warren had the *Chicago Tribune* for her, *McClure's,* another copy of the *Theatre Magazine*, another *Vogue,* the *Red Book,* the *Green Book,* the *Saturday Evening Post.* He had engaged a drawing room for her, tipped the porter to see that all went well.

The train rumbled out of Chicago, where up at Rush Street at Mrs. Newbury's she had had her first key. Chicago, where she and Eva had splurged on a Parmalee cab and the driver said, "There is no North Rush, just Rush." And where if the phone call was for her she could go down to the wall phone in her wrapper. Had Eva known about her and Rex? Known when she and Dennis? Why hadn't she and Dennis worked out? He was great about the abortion. He was great about the divorce. He was great about everything. Wouldn't it be better if she had stayed Mrs. Dennis Ryan? But could he have gotten her in the Princess show? Morty knew everybody. Now *she'd* started to be known. Not like Marion Davies or Justine Johnstone, but still, people knew Winona Lloyd.

The big somber Minneapolis Station. Her Pullman porter had a redcap for her, her train home went out of the same station. Before long, familiar stations, familiar scenes. Reminders of that first trip from Glorieta with her mother and Mrs. Brigham and the rain had poured down. It was raining today—

"Next stop, Winona," called out the conductor. It

wasn't Mr. Watson. He was younger. On the platform was George. She had never seen a man cry. He put his arms around her. She knew then without being told.

"When?"

"Night before last." The tears kept dropping.

That had been Monday, the night she set out. She was in her drawing room looking at magazines and sipping a glass of champagne the Pullman porter said a gentleman had sent her.

"The parlor clock struck twelve," said George. "She was in my arms, I could feel her breathe, then—" He couldn't go on.

"Was Dr. Jensen there?" She didn't really know what to say.

George nodded, reached for his handkerchief. "Dr. Jensen came right away, but he had expected it. The first attack was severe. Dr. Jensen knew it had to be."

"How could it? She was young. Oh, George."

"She loved you." He picked up the bags and they walked to his car. "She missed you, but she knew your life wasn't here." He drove over the railroad bridge, down Station Street to Maplewood. "You made her anxious, but she said, 'It's *her* life, she has to live it.'"

Annie Sedig opened the front door. She had come over from West Winona to help.

"Services will be at three."

"I wish I'd been better."

"She loved you. I know I said that but she loved you. Nothing shook that."

Annie was taking the bags up. "You're in *your* room."

Still with the big yellow roses on the wallpaper. Still her bamboo bookcase, the shirtwaist box her mother and

Mrs. Brigham had covered with cretonne patterned in yellow roses. "Maybe you'll like to be alone," said George. "I'm downstairs when you want me. I'll call Mrs. Penniman. She wants to come down. She and Mr. Penniman were away taking the cure at French Lick Springs in Indiana, but when I telegraphed, they telegraphed they were starting back. She wants to see you." He went downstairs.

The yellow roses in the wallpaper had hardly faded. Yellow was the color dress she wore when Larry Dineen put his hand under it to feel her breasts. Why did she tell her mother? Was it to hurt her for the closed door? She looked around. It was all the same, but she was different. The way she'd said she'd be.

For this trip she'd worn no jewelry, her plainest dress, but it didn't look plain. Madame Frances never made a plain dress and this dark blue serge with the black silk braid looked elegant and sexy and expensive when all it was, was dark blue serge. What made it Madame Frances? Was it the black braid? Black patent leather pointed shoes with French heels from Slater's and sheer silk stockings like Lily Corey's. *They* were different, but Slater shoes were all she had. For the service she had the black taffeta long-sleeved dress, V-neck, but not sexy, showed nothing. The services would be at three o'clock in the parlor. Now the doors were closed. In front of the buff brick fireplace was the dark gray coffin, open. Her mother. She kissed her. For the first time no response. Her mother. Her mother. How had they got so far apart? Mr. Flood the undertaker was placing rows of small chairs in the hall, the parlor. Beside the coffin, the couch had been lifted out to Mr. and Mrs. Roberts's around the other side of the house. Chairs were in the dining room. George and Winona and Mrs. Penniman would sit at the head of the stairs, where they could hear but not be seen. On the front door beside the big brass "41" was black crepe and purple ribbon to show a funeral was taking place.

Mrs. Penniman, looking pretty in a gray silk dress— her face seemed unchanged—took Winona in her arms and they both cried. Mrs. Penniman reached up her sleeve for the handkerchief. "I told Joe, 'She was the dearest, best person I ever knew, Joe, and I have to be truthful, that has to include you.' "

"Was he upset?"

"No indeed. He knew I was right. He knew I couldn't say that to him if it wasn't so." The telephone rang. Mrs. Penniman or Annie answered it. George was with Mr. Flood, helping. The calls were for him. Did nobody know Winona had come back? Anna? Florence? Marian? Rachel? Kitty? Louise?

"Anna married and lives out to Plainview." Mrs. Penniman was trying to make things right. "I don't suppose she knew you're back. Louise lives with her mother. I believe I heard she might be engaged. George Snowden is a dear man, Winona. No one could love someone more that he loved your mother. And do for her. He's the best. You don't know what a comfort he was when you went off to school in Chicago."

"Is Florence here?"

"Florence married and lives in Sioux City. She inherited her mother's voice and is soloist in Sioux City Congregational Church and sometimes comes here to give a concert. She'd have sung today if she'd been here. Mr.

Boynton will play 'Sweet Hour of Prayer' on the piano and 'Rock of Ages.' Long ago your mother told me that had been your father's favorite. Being a mining engineer, I guess it was a meaningful song in his business. Miss Gracia Godfrey will sing, I forget what it is, but she says your mother would like—no, wait, it's called 'Beautiful Island of Somewhere.'

"After the people leave, you and I and George will get in our car. Joe will be in front with Vernon, he's still with us. You remember our driver? Too bad it's raining, but that can't be helped."

"A lot of people will stay home," said Mr. Flood. "I'm not setting out any more chairs."

"You're so good." Winona took Mrs. Penniman's hand. "You were always so good to mama and me and I wasn't any good to you." She started to cry.

Mrs. Penniman just held her hand tight. "Have things gone all right for you?"

Winona closed her eyes, the tears pushed out. "It's what I wanted. It's what I knew I could do, but I wish it hadn't hurt mama. I guess I sound cheap, but I had to get out. She had George and he's dear, but I don't want him. I'm wicked and I like it and it seems all right to be wicked in New York, but it sounds worse than I thought it would in this parlor. I want things, I want everything. Even married to anybody rich like Mr. Penniman and nice, I wouldn't want *that.* What's the matter with me that I feel like that?"

Mrs. Penniman patted her hand. "You were never like any little girl. You were like all the little *babies,* but from when you got to be maybe as early as five, you were different."

"Maybe it was that Mr. Barney. You hated his sign, 'Garage and Implements,' remember? And I saw him doing things to Nita Macchi and I didn't know what, but I think that's what started me doing what I do. It's what I *can* do and I *do* it. I knew mama knew because I told her."

Mrs. Penniman squeezed Winona's hand. "She told me. She didn't want to tell George, but she did need comfort. She told me."

"Mrs. Brigham—I know you're not Mrs. Brigham, but Mrs. Brigham, you've all my life been my comfort."

Reverend Chase began, "Dearly beloved," he stood on the stairs by the pineapple newel post. Up in the hall sat George, Winona and Mrs. Brigham. For today she had to be Mrs. Brigham, even though she was Mrs. Penniman. Their chairs were outside the door to Winona's yellow-rose wallpapered room. Mrs. Penniman sat almost directly in front of the shirtwaist box she and Beryl had covered for Winona.

Reverend Chase's voice went on. Mr. Flood's chairs rattled whenever anybody moved. People's wet raincoats and umbrellas were left in the kitchen, their rubbers out on the covered piazza. Mr. Boynton played "Sweet Hour of Prayer." Reverend Chase led everyone in prayer. Miss Gracia Godfrey sang with Mr. Boynton accompanying her on the square piano George had bought for Winona. Winona didn't hear Miss Godfrey, she heard

> Get out and get under
> He had to get under
> To fix up his little machine.

Why think of that? That was years ago, before every-thing.

Reverend Chase spoke about Beryl. Her loss would be felt in Winona. The Lord's Prayer and Reverend Chase's blessing. It was over. People filed out. The door opened and shut. Then George and Winona and Mrs. Penniman joined Joe in the car. Vernon standing outside until Mrs. Penniman called out, "Get in, Vernon, you'll catch your death."

There was a long wait. Mr. Flood's men were carrying her mother down the steps of 41 Maplewood. The first time Winona had gone up those steps was with Rachel Dudley. Mrs. Brigham had fixed them lunch. "You'll have the first meal in the new house." Beryl and George were going to return that afternoon from their honey-moon . . . .

Mr. Flood's men, bare heads glistening in the rain, guided the gray coffin past the Winona granite hitching post that had lost its hitching ring. They eased the coffin into Mr. Flood's hearse. The engine started. Mr. Flood went back to remove the black crepe with the purple ribbon from the front door, got into the seat of the hearse. Victor followed.

Out at Mount Winona, Reverend Chase spoke a few words beside the grave, lined with rain-drenched pine boughs. George held an umbrella over Winona and him-self. Mr. and Mrs. Penniman shared theirs. Victor stood near the car beneath the car umbrella. Annie Sedig Tuo-minen shared an umbrella with her husband and that was all that came.

"It's the rain keeps people in," said Mr. Flood.

The Pennimans got into their car with George and

Winona. "We'll drop you off. You're coming to our house for dinner. Is six-thirty too early? We like to eat early."

"George." Winona looked around the parlor. The Robertses had the sofa back in its place. It all looked the same, the clock, the cherry table, the black leather chair.

"I guess I know what you're going to say, Winona."

"I feel like I'm—I feel like I'm insulting everybody if I stay here."

"Don't say that. Don't think that."

"I'm awful, George. I am, and it's the way I mean to be. Or I don't know if I'm awful, but I know I'm awful the way people think *here*. Remember Mrs. Watson in the tight-fitting suits? And her face made up and she took the 2:10 train to Minnie every Tuesday and Thursday afternoon? People said she was *terrible*. Well, I'm worse. George, help me. I'm not going to Mrs. Penniman's tonight. I'm not this life. Get me on the 5:30 to Minnie. Will you do that for me, George?"

"You really want to?"

"George, I do. All I need is you to get me on the train. I'll get out of Minnie to Chicago. George"—she couldn't go on for a minute—"understand."

"It's how you say."

She hugged him. "You know it's nothing to do with mama. She's not here and you are and you're nice, but I'm *there.*" She pointed. "That's New York, that's what I mean when I say *there.*"

Winona was halfway up the stairs. "George, I have to have a telegram go. Will you send it?"

He got out his pad marked "OLSSON'S FRUIT AND

VEGETABLES IN SEASON—RELY ON US." His pencil was blue and in white letters it read "CLAFLIN'S PRODUCE."

"George, send it to Mr. Mortimer Burrage. B-U-R-R-A-G-E. Two *R*'s. Capitol Theatre Building, 1607 Broadway, New York."

LEAVING AT FIVE-THIRTY TODAY FRIDAY STOP TAKING MINNEAPOLIS ST PAUL UNION PACIFIC SLEEPER TO CHICAGO STOP CHICAGO SATURDAY, LAKE SHORE LIMITED STOP NEW YORK SUNDAY AFTERNOON

"Sign it, 'WINONA'. "

George was writing. She ran down the two steps and hugged him. "Thank you for being so great to us. Don't think I'm a tramp, I love what I'm doing and I'm not sorry. I love to be wild, I hate being secure. Maybe I'll change, but I have to admit I hope not. Tell Annie to just give me whatever's ready." She charged up the stairs.

That part of life was over.

60

THE LAKE SHORE Limited pulled into Grand Central.
Barnes in his claret-colored chauffeur livery was at the
gate with a redcap. With the *captain* of the redcaps.
Barnes introduced him.

"It's my time to go off duty, but I consider it a privi-
lege to handle the luggage of Miss Winona Lloyd."

Winona thanked him.

"Barnes has your limousine in the private spot for
famous people's cars."

She thanked him again.

At the hotel, Barnes saw to it that a bellboy brought
her bags up. She unlocked the door and was in Morty's
arms. "Darling, darling, did you bring everything back?"
His lips were on hers, soft yet possessive. It felt beautiful. It felt like life starting again. She was where there
was no scary feeling, where it was not wicked, where it
was like it was meant to be.

A knock at the door. A bellboy came with her bags.
Morty gave him a dollar. He was gone.

"Shall I take a bath first?" How great that it was right
to be with him.

"Yes. I'll watch."

61

SHE HAD LEFT Dennis and the Hotel Algonquin for Mortimer and the luxurious four-room suite at the Hotel Claridge, then one Saturday night at the Hotel Ritz's Sixty
Club with Morty, she and Florenz Ziegfeld came together.

The Sixty Club supper and dance was elegance itself.
To belong you had to be a someone in the theatre, a
producer, playwright, actor, actress, director, scenery designer, costume designer. Outsiders might only come as
a member's guest. Originally there were sixty members,
but now it was any theatre person who could afford it.
Every other Saturday night in the Crystal Ballroom of
the Hotel Ritz, uptown west corner of Madison Avenue,
East Forty-Sixth Street, New York's most elegant hotel.
On the exciting every other Saturday night at eleven
o'clock, the orchestra played, the tables with red shaded
lamps, fringed and covered with silver lattice, shone
softly on flowers, crystal and silver. On the polished
floor stage greats wearing Wetzel or Earl Benham tux-
edos, Madame Frances's or Lucile's most sexy, dazzling
evening dresses waltzed and one-stepped. To enter the
Crystal Ballroom, what an entrance! Down a flight of

stairs, often the start of a wedding, affair, divorce, a play, a musical . . . anything could take place on a Saturday night at the Sixty Club. And did. People knew people, but it was the John Paul Jones that brought people to know people who hadn't.

"The next dance will be the John Paul Jones," announced the orchestra leader. Everybody marched, girls going forward, fellows coming toward them, everybody touching hands as they passed. Morty left Winona, went his way, Winona went hers, the orchestra stopped, whoever faced whomever were partners till next the music stopped. It stopped. Facing Winona was Florenz Ziegfeld, the king of musical comedy. His Follies made Forty-second Street's handsome New Amsterdam Theatre the place to be, the place to be seen and to see, then at midnight his Ziegfeld Frolic on the New Amsterdam Roof. Everybody knew his name, had seen his picture. Florenz Ziegfeld was Broadway.

He put his arm around Winona's pale green taffeta waist and they danced. He didn't speak, she didn't. His eyes were saying something, her eyes were answering back.

"When?" he asked.

"When you say."

"Tomorrow?"

She nodded. "Morty's daughter is coming from boarding school tomorrow."

"One o'clock, Ansonia Hotel."

The music stopped.

"One o'clock," he whispered again. The music started, he marched on.

Was this the somewhere where she always knew she

was going? The music stopped, facing her was Ray Comstock, who produced the Princess show she was in.

Morty came with her up to the Claridge suite. He
would drive back to Tarrytown to spend tomorrow with
his daughter from boarding school.

He undid the Madame Frances pale green taffeta. "Did
you like Flo?"

"He doesn't say much." Madame Frances's pale green
beauty dropped to the floor.

He fondled her. "Darling, I shall miss you tomorrow.
Come to the Capital Monday, we'll lunch." A long kiss,
he was gone.

The phone rang.

She picked up the receiver. "Hello."

"Is this a wrong number?"

Winona laughed. "It would have been two minutes
ago. Now I hope it's the right one."

"Why are you alone?"

"Morty's daughter is spending tomorrow with him.
He left for Tarrytown."

"And you've left him for me."

"I have?"

"One o'clock tomorrow, no, today. Eighth floor, the
Ansonia Hotel, turn left when you get out of the elevator, the door to Number Eighty-one will be unlocked."

62

SHE GAVE BARNES the day off, took a taxi to Seventy-fourth Street and Broadway. Through the ornate lobby, up the gilded elevator, eighth floor, turn left. Eighty-one, she turned the knob.

"Come in," came a voice from another room.

She went through the open door. On the bed in white silk pajamas was Flo Ziegfeld. His arms went around her. He held her head back and looked and looked and looked, then kissed her as though the long look had made him thirsty. "How old are you?"

"Seventeen."

"I want you."

Madame Frances's pink silk dress was off. The Boué Soeurs pink chiffon roses stopped covering anything. Flo's hand pulled the drawers aside.

Was it real? Was it her? Was this who Larry Dineen took that night under the bushes at Butler's Pond? All the things she'd learned from Dennis, would they please Florenz Ziegfeld?

He lay back on the pillow and, as they said, drank her in.

"This is your suite. Tell Morty tomorrow. He'll understand, and tell them at the Princess. You'll be in my Follies line with Jessie Reed, Lil Tashman, Kay Laurell. You'll be the new Follies beauty." He pulled her closer. "Last night at the Sixty Club did you think you'd be in bed with me?"

"I wanted to."

63

AT LUNCH with Morty she told him. He looked at her a long time, then nodded. A man of the world, he knew show business people took what they wanted. He took her hand. "Flo can do everything for you. I shall miss you, darling."

Winona leaned over and kissed him. "You've been great to me, Morty." She offered him her lips.

"When do you want to leave the Claridge?"

"Tomorrow? Flo has a place for me at the Ansonia."

"Take everything, of course, everything is yours. I'll come to see you in the Follies and think of things we've done together. And the three freckles. I wish I were competition."

"Morty, I was crazy about you."

"Yes, darling, but you're seventeen and I'm seventy.

And yesterday in Tarrytown I spent Sunday with my daughter. It was her birthday, she was seventeen yesterday."

64

THE TOWER SUITE was Winona's. The tower suite below was Mr. and Mrs. Ziegfeld's. February, Mrs. Billie Burke Ziegfeld spent in Palm Beach.

In tower suite 81 Ziegfeld didn't wait for nighttime. Sometimes in the sitting room Eddie Schmidt, his bookkeeper, would wait for him. He had come to bring the figures Ziegfeld needed. The bedroom door was closed, but Eddie knew what was going on. Sounds let him know Winona Lloyd was good. The girls said all Ziegfeld cared about was himself. Winona was making him care. Also making it on the New Amsterdam Roof in the Midnight Frolic. In the big flower-trimmed, beribboned swing she swung out over the audience. Downstairs in the New Amsterdam in the Follies she did the showgirl walk across the stage, drawing the French blue velvet curtain. Around her downstage leg was a blue velvet loop, her bare bottom and bare leg moving slowly drew the French blue velvet curtain with it.

Getting the loop around her leg, house carpenter

Nolan had to adjust the curtain so that the whole leg and half her pink bottom showed, but no red curls. His hand took a quick feel. "Can I get in there?" he whispered.

She shrugged. Why? She was Flo's when he had time, but somebody young? Somebody *young*.

"Afternoon?" He adjusted the blue velvet curtain, same color as the blue velvet drapes at Auntie Cora's and Auntie Belle's.

A soft persuasive hand. No rough thumb. "My place?"

A whisper. "I'll have a hair appointment."

"The Landseer, corner West Fifty-second and Eighth Avenue."

65

THE APARTMENT was one room, the apartment house was third rate, but not Mac Nolan. No rush. Ziegfeld always had a lot to do and to get to, to go to. Not Mac Nolan. He was slow. He was a tease. He was great, knew he was great and enjoyed being great. Took his time, was the boss.

"Mac?" She was pleading. "Mac, do it."

He laughed. Ziegfeld's girl begging the show's carpenter for it.

Four times was the record one Thursday.

She held her face up and whispered, "Again?"

Mac kissed her pretty places. "I could, but I'm leaving one for Ziegfeld."

66

AT REUBEN'S for scrambled eggs after the Sixty Club, movie star Jack Bedford came over to Ziegfeld's table. In the movies Winona was crazy about him. He was handsome, young, wicked looking. His wife had been a chorus girl in the Follies, then in Paris she swallowed acid. Had she meant to? Anyway, she was dead. Ziegfeld didn't like him.

That didn't bother Jack. He sat down. "We never met," he said to Winona, kissed her, got up and left.

"Steer clear of him. Ruin sets in when he goes for a girl. He hangs around the Frolic and he's good-looking and a movie star so some of the girls go for him. A movie star, they think that's copacetic! Nobody smart does, but he got Avis Tobey. Ever see her? Lovely! Fanny Brice tried to straighten her out, but he had her on the sniff-sniff. Fanny couldn't get anywhere with her. Jack married the kid and one night in Paris at the Ritz she drank half a bottle of acid and writhed her way out of life."

"How awful. Oh, how *awful.*"

"Let's get out of here. Thinking about Avis has me spinning down. Sweetie, come home, make me feel what it's like when it goes right."

67

IT WAS IN Winchell's column that Ziegfeld had joined Billie Burke in Palm Beach. The phone rang. It was Jack Bedford. "Want to go stepping?"

Winona thought about Avis and that awfulness, but he was so attractive.

He took her to the Lido, a dark corner table. "Put your satchel here," he told Winona and pointed at the chair. Jack took a crazy look at her and gave her something.

"What do I do with it?" Nobody had ever shown her the white stuff.

He helped her sniff it. Showed her the tricks. He was young. Nobody young since Dennis, and some afternoons with Mac. The white stuff worked, it made everything seem great but wasn't everything great? This was new. Maybe try it?

"Wouldn't be without it," Jack kept saying. The orchestra played Jerome Kern's "I'm just a wild rose, just a prim and mild rose."

Sniff, sniff.

The room looked even more beautiful. Her Milgrim cloth-of-gold dress with the overdress of yellow organdy with tomato-red ribbons looked even more beautiful than when Ellie put it over her head and she slithered into it.

"You want to stay here or come up to my place and show me your old tomato?"

Why did she get helpless with laughter? Why did everything seem to zip? It was like riding on the Twentieth Century, racing the world outside and winning.

"Want to show me your old tomato *here?*"

She couldn't stop laughing. "Stop it!"

"Let's dance and make everybody wonder why we're not at my place doing it." He took her hand, she was in his arms foxtrotting like the Castles over at Castle House. Were they as beautiful as they thought they were?

Yes, they were. Would she and Jack do it beautifully up to his place?

Yes, they would.

He laid her on the floor.

"It's too hard," she complained, but he didn't listen. Was it the sniff, sniff?

"If you had Flo and me laid side by side and you had to choose, would you say 'Eeny, meeny, miney, mo, into me this guy will go'? Would you rather me or Flo?"

Dennis had been great, but not wild. Was it the sniff, sniff?

No worry if Flo rang up the tower suite, she and Peggy Hopkins had an arrangement that they'd gone out with

Peggy's friend Roger Davis, a pansy, but so funny everybody liked to be around with him.

68

Ziegfeld came back from Palm Beach. Billie Burke Ziegfeld stayed. Was he different? Was he? What was it? He did all the things but was he different?

The grapevine said he had made Marilyn Miller. Had he? Why hadn't it happened before? She was in his latest show, called "Sally." Why would it take this long? They said the grapevine is never wrong, but who knows what's the real grapevine? It was probably not the real.

Winona was in Flo's arms, there was no Marilyn. He lay back and moaned, "You're beautiful, even with the curse. How much longer?"

"Maybe tomorrow."

69

Was ziegfeld cheating on her? The phone didn't ring, the key didn't rattle in the door. Midnight. Half past. One o'clock. Was he with his wife or was he laying his great star Marilyn Miller? When she had been married to young musical comedy star Harry Porter, she didn't look at anyone, then came the awful night when Harry was driving from Pittsburgh, where his show had closed, to Chicago to meet Marilyn, playing in the Follies. Harry was driving a dashing red Stutz, it missed a curve and neither it nor Harry spent Christmas with Marilyn. The Christmas present killed Harry. Marilyn sobbed and sobbed, knew there was no more life for her. She was twenty, dreaded living without Harry, but after lots more success, lots of attention, she managed to find comfort.

Outside the New Amsterdam stage door, a shiny pearl-gray limousine, *MM* on the door. On the hubcap, the silver head of the goddess Minerva, after whom the car was named. Minerva, goddess of wisdom, is it wise to take what's handed out? Ziegfeld had given the car to Marilyn. He gave one just like it, except for the letters on the door, to himself.

One o'clock in the tower suite, Winona listened for the phone, the key in the door. Waiting was new. Waiting for a man, new. What do girls do who have to wait? What do girls do at one o'clock without a fellow? Was Flo dropping her the way he had dropped Jessie Reed for Olive Thomas, dropped *her* for—the list went on and on. Billie Burke, did she—the phone, Flo's voice, "Tied up tonight. Sorry, darling." His voice was gone. Where? Tied up where? With whom? His wife? Call down to her? Ask? Do girls call up wives? Ask Billie what *she* does when Flo's two-timing *her?* Does Billie know about Flo and her? Does she care? Did Eva Dill hate it when Rex was making excuses? Did Eva wait for the phone call, did she listen for the key in the door those afternoons Rex was at the pay-by-the-afternoon inside room at the old Virginia Hotel? Tonight was Flo cheating on her? *Was* he? Did that mean *take* it? Did it mean maybe remember who had looked at her and kept hands-off Flo Ziegfeld's girl? Maybe it was time to hook on to a Hearst, like Marion? Not Jack Bedford. Great, but unreliable. Did the Ansonia bedroom have a transient look? Not transient like the Virginia Hotel, and yet underneath the frills did it look like a place for a beauty? Then a new beauty? Then on and on till out-of-date?

Flo and Marilyn, where would *they?* Marilyn's sister lived with her in the apartment. Marilyn, a charmer, a dazzler, young, loved to laugh. Did Flo laugh? Did he? You didn't think of him as a laugher, he was for sex, beauty, his Follies, his Frolic, his "Sally," "Sunny," "Rosalie." Marilyn would love taking him away from Winona Lloyd, then once hers, would it wear out? She was blonde and adorable and liked young and fun.

Jack Bedford could be Marilyn's kind, she'd go for the stuff. Did she like being bruised up by sexy movie star Jean Manueldo? Her maid had had to put makeup over the black-and-blue spots so they wouldn't show for the matinee. Besides batting her around, he'd thrown her diamond-and-ruby bracelet down the toilet and pulled the chain. Her maid Selina had to get the engineer up. But never mind Marilyn, did Winona need Flo? She'd made her name, she could stay in the Follies, be on the roof, her picture was in the rotogravure sections. Alfred Cheney Johnson's photograph of her rear view, sepia brown and soft and ready, had become famous. The three freckles showed.

The Follies stars were Fanny Brice, Ed Wynn, Leon Errol, Joe Frisco, Marilyn, Ann Pennington, but star attractions were the beauties—Texas Jessie Reed, blonde Helen Lee Worthing, Lil Tashman, Kay Laurell, Peggy Hopkins, Lillian Lorraine, Carmelita Geraghty. The grapevine said Flo had had them all, but were *they* sitting around waiting? The grapevine said Lillian would make Flo wait to drive him crazy. So why was Winona Lloyd waiting for *him?* She was younger than any of them. Men liked young, especially if they were young and could. Virgins were an excitement to start, then they hated to be hurt, and why was that blood stuff so great?

Winona was twenty, still wanting to learn, but Larry Dineen was the only one she hadn't pleased. Well, he hadn't pleased *her.* Who would be good to change to? Morty was out of the running, he'd got married to the boarding-school roommate of his daughter. Beautiful, seventeen, no money, from Brooklyn Heights. Her adorable blonde beauty was what her family had to sell. Would anybody believe seventeen married to seventy-three and madly in love with him? They had a baby. My God, what a thought. She could have got pregnant by Morty and had to have another abortion. Who could have thought to be careful with *him?* They said his wife loved the baby, but couldn't wait for Mortimer Burrage to do it to her. *Maybe* with some help he could do it twice. Never mind, he made her starry-eyed. Her family was also starry-eyed, the money they'd invested in her paid off, boarding school where rich girls go and where Dolly Burrage invited her to spend Easter week with her and her father at the apartment over the Capitol Theatre. When night came and after his daughter got to bed he'd come in for a good-night kiss and cuddle, and then after that he went in to Caroline, kissed her good night and the same cuddle only a little bit more so. For a virgin it opened up life.

Was Morty home with her tonight in Tarrytown or was she waiting, too? Doing it with a virgin wouldn't be exciting for a whole year unless she caught on and got over it. Might Morty have married Winona? Might that have been good? And was what she was doing good? From Glorieta to grown-up in the town of Winona to all she learned in Chicago and if she wrote down her occupation, she'd have to write, "Men." How else could she get money? She could make beds, she could dust and sweep, she couldn't wait on tables, she couldn't sew, she couldn't cook. Mrs. Brigham had said, "Want me to start you with a two-egg yellow cake?" How far away all that from the pale-blue Ansonia tower bedroom. Beryl and George and Mrs. Brigham—no—Mrs. Penniman. They thought she was wrong, but life on Johnson Avenue, on Sanburn Street, on Maplewood, wasn't for her. Was she doing what Auntie Cora and Auntie Belle did to get things? She had a lot of money from Morty, diamonds from Flo, and her salary every week that Eddie Schmidt brought round to her dressing room and didn't knock. Her maid Ellie bawled him out because he said he didn't have time to knock, and while he was saying so he took a good look at Winona.

"She hasn't got anything on!" yelled Ellie.

"Sign here." Eddie put the salary sheet down on the makeup.

"She hasn't got anything on."

"I have, I got a hard-on. Give me back my pencil." He took it and he and salary list were out the door—

Suddenly she was crying. Flo was cheating, but was she cheating on herself? What could she do? Rachel was a schoolteacher. Florence got married right after High and continued her singing, she had a good voice. Winona could sing, but nobody'd say she could live on it. Anna went to Vassar College and got married and had a kid. What would *she* do with a kid? She stopped crying. "Be tough," she told herself, "You're not a homemaker, what about Julius Schwab?" His eyes had glistened at the Ritz Crystal Ballroom Sixty Club when Jack Bedford took her to Mr. Hearst's Valentine party for Marion. What about Julius Schwab? He owned everything and spent. Poured it out for opera singer Mary Grace, then she married Jose Calendro. Who said, "Never leave a millionaire for a tenor?" But Mary did. Had Julius been hooked by anyone yet? Next morning ring up Kuhn, Loeb. Next morning might have its own story to tell. If Flo snuck into bed later with a good excuse, well—If Flo was with Marilyn, Kuhn, Loeb might just be the right investment.

70

JULIUS SCHWAB was made happy. He set Winona up in a four-story granite house on Riverside Drive. She had a cook, maid, butler. Right after New Year's Julius took her to Palm Beach. January, 1926. He was taking her on his private railroad car, "The Elsewhere." Rich, rich, great supporter of the arts, a Maecenas, a power, cultured, a few years younger than Morty.

At Palm Beach, early evenings at Bradley's for gambling. Only for pleasure, to pass the time until he brought her back to his pink palace. Outside her windows a walled heliotrope garden laid out in designs. Mrs. Brigham had planted a row of heliotrope in the border underneath the parlor windows at Maplewood Avenue. The fragrance from Julius Schwab's pink walled garden floated up to the bed where she lay in Julius's arms. Doing it with Julius, the heliotrope perfume brought her back to the worrisome closed doors with George and Beryl inside and the bed creaking, and Mrs. Brigham, now Joseph Penniman's Allie, in the big white house with the columns. Mr. Penniman must be even older than Julius. Julius was asleep. Did Mr. Penniman fall asleep after doing it with Mrs. Brigham?

What about George? Did he live in the house alone? Maybe write to him? Maybe not. So much not to say. And who lived in the Sanburn Street house after Mrs. Brigham moved out? Was the hammock on the back porch? Did anyone watch the Holbrook boys? One time she went over and played ball, the younger one carried her home piggyback. Did they still live there?

Everything all right, then a Western Union boy delivered a telegram to the pink house with the heliotrope flowers. Mrs. Schwab was ready to begin her season in Palm Beach.

The Elsewhere was dispatched to New York.

Julius arranged for a suite for Winona at the Poinciana Hotel. Helen Lee Worthing was there, and Peggy Hopkins. Like Winona, they left the Follies when they had anything more fun to do and of course always when it went on tour. Flo was in the house he'd rented for Billie and himself. It looked over the Everglades Club.

Winona's suite was on the same floor at the Poinciana where Harry Daugherty was paying Helen Lee's bills. "Want to race Winona and Peggy?" he asked Helen. "Down the hall to the window, no clothes and for the winner!" He flashed a crisp new ten thousand dollar bill. "Where do we start?" asked Peggy.

"From here." He opened the door to his suite. "Everybody get their chastity belt off."

Helen started ripping off her New York Milgrim pink sports crepe de chine. Peggy, down to her lace-and-blue-ribbon garter belt. Winona hadn't worn any underwear, her red dotted silk Madame Frances was on the floor.

Harry opened his sitting room door and the three raced down the corridor. Can luck be rotten! Outside suite B-14 the old, gray-haired security guard appeared and put a stop to the race.

"This is a resort hotel," said Harry. "We're resorting to sports! Get yourself canned, spoil sport!"

The three graces did their showgirl walk past him and Harry roared with laughter. "Take a glass of champagne, girls, wet your whistle, not your pants. Oh, you left them here. Everybody gets ten thousand dollars, but you have to, everybody, do it with me. You first, Peggy, we never met in the sack." His pants were off, Peggy down beside him. "Winona and Helen, watch and see what you can pick up from Peggy." He and Peggy got lost. Two experts, acting as though they weren't. Also appreciating real talent.

Then Helen, for whom he was paying all her bills, no novelty.

Then Winona. They liked it. "For a wife, Julius takes a chance on you at the Poinciana? Out of his famous art collection, can't he spare a chastity belt? Girls, you only cost me thirty thousand dollars, *I'm* the winner."

No worry about Julius. In his pink palace he and frost-bitten Mrs. Julius Schwab entertained the Stotesburys, the Guinesses, Lord and Lady Royden, Lady Astor, Mr. and Mrs. Charles Dana Gibson. After dinner Joseph Hoffman played.

Over at the Poinciana, Harry was laying Winona. Playing the field were Peggy and Helen but all joined up for a fun occasion. At the pink palace Mrs. Schwab was staying on so Julius went back to New York on

The Elsewhere. Winona in the drawing room of the adjoining car, just in case Mrs. Schwab should come to The Elsewhere to say goodbye. Fat chance.

Lying beside Julius in the private car she wore her emerald bracelet, emerald necklace with the emerald cross, cabochon emerald ring, souvenirs from Palm Beach's Worth Avenue.

"I'm tired tonight, darling," said Julius. "Tomorrow we'll be going through South Carolina. At least I'll be the first to have you in the Carolinas. Well, won't I?"

She just smiled.

71

THE ANNUAL board meeting of the Pittsburgh Carnegie Museum of Arts was scheduled. Late afternoon Julius and Winona boarded The Elsewhere waiting on a private rail at Penn Station in New York. Next day before the meeting they lunched at Pittsburgh's Union League Club. Who was the elegant, distinguished beauty attracting attention? She stopped at their table. Mrs. Alexander Moore shook hands with Julius. "You're dining with us," she reminded him, then looked at Winona. "You look like someone I knew a long time ago. A pretty girl in a musical comedy I was in."

"At Weber and Fields' my mother acted with you. Her name was Beryl White."

"Did she leave the stage?"

"She married my father in Hancock, Michigan, and they made their home in New Mexico. In Glorieta. He died before I was born. He was a mining engineer. Mama and I lived there until I was five when we moved to Winona in Minnesota."

"And I'm from Council Bluffs in Iowa." For some reason she laughed. "Come to dinner with Julius tonight. How pretty you are!"

Winona looked startled. "Oh, thank you, but what will I wear?"

"You'll find everything at Mr. Kaufman's Department Store, third floor. They have Poiret, Vionnet, Lanvin, a few Milgrims, and even a few Madame Franceses. With your figure you'll step into any of them."

The Alexander Moore mansion was elegance itself. He was wealthy, had been ambassador to Spain. He had married the beautiful Lillian Russell, who knew all about how to do everything, including run a mansion. Did she learn in her Diamond Jim Brady days? Days and nights with Howard Gould? Then Alexander Moore from Pittsburgh, her beauty knocked him cold. Her style, what was it? Where did it come from? Diamond Jim? Shy Howard? Not Council Bluffs. Or did it? That's where it had its roots, where the fine ladies of Council Bluffs made an art of respectability, rather than a bore.

Twenty guests, Winona counted. The twenty guests counted her. Mr. Kaufman's third floor had enhanced her with a Lanvin black chiffon, outlining her figure without hinting what could happen underneath.

"You need different jewelry," said Mrs. Moore, as she welcomed Winona in the drawing room. She spoke to the butler, "Have Rosalie bring down my jewel case."

Presto! "Rosalie, put her string of emeralds in here." Rosalie unclasped Winona's necklace.

"Emeralds don't go with black. Rosalie will give it back when you go. *Pearls* with your poitrine. Pearls, the emerald ring is fine. No bracelets. You're a real beauty. What do you do with it besides Julius?"

"I'm in the Follies."

"You swung out in the Frolic swing. I remember. Red hair you don't forget."

At table she sat between an elderly, distinguished Mr. Somebody, definitely a somebody, and Sir Frederick Malleson. They talked across her about flat racing and harness racing. Sir Frederick had a hackney pony, champion of England for four years straight. Mr. Somebody had his breeding farm in Kentucky. He bred flatracers and jumpers. His mare Alita won him fame and more money.

"Are you interested in racing?" he asked Winona.

"I never went to a race."

"Oh," said Sir.

"Is that so?" said Mister.

That wound up the conversation. Talk, talk, talk between the gentlemen, then Winona thought she'd try something. "I go to polo."

"Ah, yes."

"*Do* you?"

Polo was of no interest. Her beauty brought her no attention.

The table made her think of long-ago Auntie Cora and

183

Auntie Belle. Silver, crystal, candles, a centerpiece of red-and-white-striped camelias flown up from the Moore plantation in South Carolina, small bunches of white bouvardia in front of each lady's place. Spirea and maidenhair fern lay here and there on the noble white damask cloth, patterned in fleurs-de-lis and embroidered *LRM*.

Coffee was served in Rockingham china, a pattern of red and gold on white. They were served as though they were demitasse cups, but they were like a small breakfast-size, a man or a lady could have as much or leave what she didn't want.

All the black ties and evening dresses sipped coffee, talking to left, then to right. Winona's left and right talked across her.

"I have a problem with Johnny-jump-up. Do you know that field weed?"

"Johnny jump?"

"Johnny-jump-up," said Winona, "It's got a little blue flower and smells funny."

Both guests looked at her in astonishment. It was as though they had no idea she was there. Beauty and dazzle didn't count in Pittsburgh? Did she have to make it on weeds?

"Johnny-jump-up grows all over the place in Minnesota. Winona, Minnesota, is where I came from. You had to weed it out if you didn't want it. I never thought it was bad, but then I like dandelions and most people dig them up."

"I see."

"In England, we have a heavy growth of vetch if we're not careful."

Mister nodded. "Vetch. I know about it, but it's not native to Kentucky."

At the foot of the table where Mrs. Alexander Moore sat straight as a statue, no thought of her back resting against the red-and-gold-brocaded, unpolished mahogany chair, the butler was offering a gold tray on which were things that looked to Winona like what was on her own makeup table at the New Amsterdam Theatre. Powder with the top off the box, flat powderpuff with a small pink bow, small rabbit's foot to brush the powder off, small gold pot of lip rouge with a ruby on the top of the cover, a golden ruby-handled brush to apply it. An ivory brush to smoothe Mrs. Moore's eyebrows, a small gold box of pale blue powder for the eyelids. How old was Mrs. Moore? Was she sixty? Was she more? Her poitrine was like a painting, rising out of gold-colored satin, matching the perfectly marcelled head. An impressive collar of rubies, and on her left hand a band of square diamonds looked too weighty to lift, but not so. The hand, its long, pink fingernails, with moon-shaped white crescents, accepted the rich brown cigar that her butler offered her. She snipped it with the gold scissors, put it between those luscious red lips, which must have once accepted Diamond Jim's. Her butler lit the cigar. Mrs. Moore had come a long way, had made use of it and didn't look it.

Winona studied her. Something to learn. Someone at least forty years older. She must have had thoughts of her future, must have looked after herself. She was a beauty, she was desirable, didn't that have to be planned for? Winona, one ear listening to flat racing and the first Belmont run in 1876, reviewed her own twenty years.

What would twenty more bring her? She was a *now* person. *Now* was what counted. If *now* was right, why wouldn't *now* be right, right on? If you knew what you were doing, what you wanted, and if you did what you did and knew how, why not expect that to go on? Had Lillian Russell gotten a lot of stocks from Diamond Jim? From Howard Gould? From whomever? Winona had been lucky. She'd never asked for it, but Morty and Flo, well, not Flo, Flo had given her jewelry, paid for the tower suite. Julius? Yes. Art and stocks and bonds. He had been lavish. Her broker's report was a treat. Had Lillian Russell the talent for men *and* for money? She must have. Winona looked toward the end of the table. The soft candlelight. That straight back. That low-cut poitrine, the ruby collar, the gold satin, lighting her like footlights. The cigar held gracefully yet professionally. The remarkable lady who had captured tycoon Alexander Moore, diplomat, ambassador to Spain . . .

"Good night, good night." Mrs. Moore's pearls went back in her jewel case and Rosalie fastened the emerald necklace and cross around Winona's neck. Good night, good night. "How much you look like your mother. What was her last name?"

"White."

"Her real name, or stage?"

"Her real."

Mrs. Moore leaned over and kissed her. "You bring back lost memories."

Julius and she got into the Moore's limousine and headed for the private car siding of Pittsburgh's Union Station.

"That dress took you away from me. I know what's under and I want it back."

Billy Joyner, The Elsewhere's steward, had the champagne in the ice bucket, bottles of French Vichy, Poland water, glasses, small pâté sandwiches, a bowl of pink peaches.

"Good night, Mr. Schwab, good night, Miss Lloyd." Billy was gone.

Julius stood at the bedroom door. "Off with that dress." Off it came. He kissed each breast. "Peaches out there. Peaches here. Lie down, darling. Make me happy."

72

IT WAS A cool night for June. The fire was lit in the bedroom's adorable pink marble fireplace, logs burning. Julius was getting into his clothes. "This weekend you're coming to Cold Spring Harbor. It'll be interesting. Some interesting people. Some you've heard of. Once a year I invite my friend Mr. Alexander Woollcott to invite some of his friends for a weekend. They come on Saturday afternoon and leave after dinner on Sunday. You'll be entertained. His list this year is Mr. Harpo Marx, Mrs. Alice Duer Miller, Miss Neysa McMein, Gregory Kelly, and his wife, an actress Ruth Gordon. Oh, and Miss McMein's husband, Mr. Jack Baragwanath." He leaned over and kissed her belly button. "Did anyone tell you you have the mound of Venus and the brown beauty spot is in a classic place?"

Winona reached out her arms for him. "Why do you have to go?"

"You sound like a little girl. I'm glad you're not." He touched her. "It wants me but tonight I have to go to a ball where nobody wants anybody. They only want to be seen." He picked up the house phone. "George, send it up, please."

"What?" asked Winona.

"A glass of champagne, a thin caviar sandwich, for you when I say good-bye."

Winona pulled the pink-chiffon-and-ribbon blanket cover over her.

George put the tray by the bed.

"Tell my car I'm coming down."

George left. Julius went over to the bed. "Let me see it." She pulled the spread aside. He kissed the red curls. Then her red mouth. "You know, my darling, I am able to solve many difficult problems, to make important decisions, but which place I love to be close to, I am not able to make a decision." He opened the door. "Tomorrow I'll tell you about Saturday and the weekend."

73

Four o'clock Saturday. Winona's limousine dropped her at the New York Yacht Club pier over on the East River, around Twenty-eighth Street.

"Good afternoon." The captain of Julius Schwab's cabin cruiser, *Undine*, was on the dock. Aboard were two ladies and Mr. Alexander Woollcott. She'd seen his picture in the paper. She'd heard him on the radio.

"You're beautiful, I must say," he said, "And I must say I'm Woollcott." He pointed to the two ladies with him. "These ladies are no competition. This is Mrs. Alice Duer *D-U-E-R* Miller, also a beauty, also in the Social Register."

"Alec!" reproved Alice Miller.

"Do you want me to bat you? If not, don't interrupt. And try to make a reasonably good impression on Miss Lloyd. Now, where was I? Ready, Miss Lloyd, we'll go on. The lady is also your senior and making a fortune writing books."

"Hello," Alice said to Winona.

"Hello." What else was she going to say?

He pointed to Ruth Gordon. "And this withered ingenue you may have seen on the stage. Ruth Gordon, married to Gregory Kelly, who is everybody's idea of charming. Today he's playing a matinee and a night performance, as is Harpo Marx, another charmer, another guest. Mr. Schwab has a car waiting in New York to speed them down here just as the evening will be wearing thin." He turned to Alice. "Why does Neysa have to be late?"

"Perhaps it's because we're early."

"Captain, what bells are we now?"

"Beg pardon, Mr. Woollcott?"

"I'm not a seafaring man, but in the books about ships when they tell time it's always eight bells. Or is it different aboard a member of the New York Yacht Club's boat?"

"Acky!" It was Neysa's throaty voice, plainsounding as when she left Quincy, Illinois, where Mrs. Raoul Fleischmann was still Ruth Gardiner, richest girl in Quincy, Illinois, and where Mary Astor was still Ella Mahaffey and Neysa was still Marjorie Glenny. That was before the numerologist told her that to succeed she must take Neysa McMein for her name, which she did, and after living six months on popcorn and a lot of water to make the popcorn swell up so she wouldn't feel like she was starving, she and her roommate Solita Solano—what numerologist took care of her?—left their dark damp studio in the Lincoln Arcade building and moved on to fame and fortune.

"Why haven't I done a cover of you?" asked Neysa of Winona.

"Don't ask stupid questions, Puss. You haven't done a cover of her because either Hearst couldn't get her to pose for you and his *Cosmopolitan* magazine or because she doesn't need a portrait. She *is* a portrait. Here's Jack."

A handsome, dark-haired tall man came aboard.

"Take off, captain," directed Woollcott, "such as we are, we're all here."

Julius would meet them at his dock in Cold Spring Harbor on Long Island. A lovely sparkly day. Winona could never get used to all this water, having Glorieta and Minnesota as her background. The Mississippi River was big, but it didn't look endless like Long Island Sound.

"Didn't I see you in the Follies?" Jack Baragwanath asked.

"I wish I could paint you with that blue velvet curtain," sighed Neysa.

"I'd like to have that." Jack smiled at Winona.

"Where do you come from?" asked Woollcott.

Alice laughed. "Alec thinks everybody has an interesting story if they just tell about themselves and where they came from."

"I don't think it's interesting, I was born in Glorieta in New Mexico."

Woollcott turned to the others. "See what I mean? You'd think I would at least have heard of the place, but I don't think they've got a radio station. I'll look into it."

"I never knew anybody born in New Mexico," mused Neysa.

"You never knew any Indians?" Woollcott looked at her, astonished. "A likely story!" To Winona, "Why were you born there? What were your people doing?"

"My mother was an actress playing one-night stands and she played one called Hancock in Michigan and met my father who was a mining engineer."

Woollcott looked at Ruth Gordon. "Did the cat get your tongue? You always inferred you were queen of the one-nighters."

"I'm listening."

Woollcott nodded. "One of the first rules of conversation."

"I'm listening and remembering when I was in a one-night stand company in *Fair and Warmer.* I had my hair Miss Lloyd's color, only mine was from henna at a Marinello Beauty Parlor in Portage, Wisconsin."

"None of your vintage memoirs! Except that you played Zona Gayle's hometown, they're not even faintly interesting. You could have improved your brain, if you *had* one at that period, which is anybody's guess, and met Zona Gayle, Portage's celebrated writer, instead of hanging around the railroad station to see what was new coming in."

"I did not. I went to the Portage department store and picked up a great remnant—it was pale green satin."

"You may be telling the truth. Zona told me Portage was noted for *her* and its remnant counter."

The boat headed into Cold Spring Harbor. On the dock was Julius Schwab to receive his guests.

Woollcott and Neysa talked about a game of croquet. "Do you play, Miss Lloyd?"

"I did when I was a little girl."

"That gives you a chance to sit on the sidelines and watch us if you don't talk. If you talk, sneeze, cheer, or boo, you wait for dinner in your room."

"I wish *my* room were next to yours, Miss Lloyd," said Jack Baragwanath.

Woollcott studied him. "Probably Neysa does too. She and Harpo plan to shack up when midnight strikes and since he and Gregory won't be able to get here till midnight strikes several times, the least we can do is try to keep Neysa awake so she won't miss her assignation. Ruth, have you booked anyone tonight? If Gregory wouldn't play havoc with these old limbs, I'd choose you to snuggle up with."

Servants in white jackets set up lawn tables and served tea, coffee, iced or hot, paper-thin sandwiches, small pink and chocolate cakes. Winona had the odd sense she was at the Baptist Strawberry Festival in West Winona. It was like it, only there the people wouldn't have been well known or showing off.

Julius sat watching the game with her and Jack Baragwanath. Not a hint of his and Winona's relationship. He behaved as though she was a niece whom he liked but did not see often. Neysa and Alice were teamed up against Alec and Ruth. They were mighty except for Ruth. "Yoked to a clod," was how Woollcott referred to his partner. Everybody knew he was crazy about her, everybody knew he wanted to marry her if she and Gregory broke up. Everybody knew she was having an affair that was serious, but they also knew the gent was seriously married. Never mind. "The ass may speak," said Woollcott, "only an old quote, nothing even faintly suggestive, but could be faintly true. All right, my siren of a fat man's unlawful bed, will you please put your ball through these two wickets or I shall get your sidekick Lou McGuire to give *The Daily Mirror* a minute-by-minute reportage of yours and her accomplishments in Palm Beach, where a certain millionaire publisher of unreadable trash offered you a thousand dollars to spend the night with him while you turned over in your so-called mind the possibility of accepting or raising the ante. Does that bring an expression to that charming face of yours, which doesn't have an instinct as to where or how a ball goes through a wicket?"

Croquet was over, everybody went to their room. Julius had arranged that Winona be in the same wing as the Woollcott party.

74

WITH JULIUS she had a lot of time to herself. Always the day, a lot of nights. He was generous and her stockbroker's account showed it, her checking account, her jewelry case, but what about that time to fill up? The only fellow she could have around was Roger Davis, who really belonged to Fanny Brice. Roger could be safe company, and who could be more entertaining? He'd dish, he'd go off into making up scenes, "That Theatre Guild lady wants to have me play Bottom, nothing personal, it's Shakespeare's, not mine, in *Midsummer Night's Dream*, and I'd just as soon, but I *must* be dressed by Erma Maloof, you know her Madison Avenue shop? Those divine tea gowns and maybe they don't suit Jacques or is that in *As You Like It?* which she wants me to play as a sister piece. Y'know, the Guild has the subscription list, so what do they care what they do to subscribers?"

He was fun. Then she liked Peggy Hopkins, now Joyce, except Mr. Joyce had lately found greener pastures or just had taken off and gone. Peggy didn't seem downhearted and she and Winona and Roger, if Fanny wasn't using him, would lunch on Delmonico's roof.

One day Charlie Dillingham came over to the table. "Why don't you two charmers be in my new show, *The Albany Nightboat,* starring Louise Grody?"

"When are rehearsals?" asked Winona.

"Two weeks from yesterday. Why don't you try it? You know me, if you want to be off you can. I'd just like to see you open, then play any performance you can. Winona, I get ants in my pants when I look at you. Maybe you'll let me make it?"

"What about me?" asked Peggy.

"You're a married lady. I don't do duels since I was forty."

Going home in her beautiful French limousine, Winona thought about it. Should she ask Julius?

Lying on the peach-colored satin sheets that night, Winona asked would he let her.

Julius was tying his tie, "Why not, my darling? I will be a stage-door Johnnie and I will be the only one who *knows* the answer. When I send the orchids with a note saying 'May I tonight?' your maid will say, 'Please go to seven-twelve Riverside Drive to her townhouse.' And I will be with adorable you."

75

IT ALL WORKED out. *The Albany Nightboat* was a big hit. Louise Grody was great to everybody. It was fun being backstage again. Beautiful clothes. Fun to wear them, fun to feel fellows wishing for you. Charlie Dillingham said, "I know you've got a 'Do Not Enter' sign, but couldn't I just deliver a package to the back door and instead of a tip, get in?

Charlie was cute and fun but not serious. He just liked to look interested, he had a beautiful wife who used to be a showgirl and who now was more interested in society than in Charlie.

One of Louise Grody's guys that looked hopeful was Archie Thayer, San Francisco's top millionaire.

Louise went for him, then selected another fellow.

"Want to go around with me?" Archie asked Winona. "You like rich old birds? Why don't you give Julius back to his wife and play ball with me? Why not loop the loop and end up in *my* bed? 'Who's been sleeping in my bed?' I'll ask and answer, 'Winona who worked it out with old Mr. Dollars.' "

Archie was maybe forty but looked young and was full of the devil. Nobody knew how much money he had.

The answer was yes.

Julius was swell. Paid off bountifully. Maybe, was he a little relieved? Busy with opera, busy with business, society and Mrs. Schwab's demands. He gave Winona the Riverside Drive house, one hundred thousand dollars in cash, United States Steel preferred stock, plus all the jewels, the emeralds from Worth Avenue, *plus* the small French limousine, black, covered with cane that reminded Winona of the cane-bottomed rocker her mother and George had bought for the kitchen of the Maplewood Avenue house and how when her mother was sick Annie Sedig used to sit and rock in it.

It was all settled and Winona belonged to Archie Thayer.

The Riverside Drive house was sold and she moved into his beautiful penthouse on Fifth Avenue atop the building Archie owned.

He was fun, he was great in bed. No evenings were better. He was separated from his wife, so they could cut out in any direction.

"Get out of the show. Come out to San Francisco with me," urged Archie. "You had enough wildcatting."

Winona did. Archie set her up in a beautiful lavish apartment on Nob Hill, overlooking the Pacific's green ships going out to Japan, green ships coming into port. Boats of all colors, going in all directions. She was crazy about Archie and living with him in San Francisco.

But it hurt Archie's wife Catherine. Badly. She killed herself. Archie hadn't lived with her for a year. Did she hope he would come back to her? Did she lose hope because of Winona? Why want a fellow who wants

197

someone else? Get another fellow that wants you or just do it with anybody you felt like it, but Archie's wife was proper, social, so she took the gun, put an end to it. Why was that proper? Why was that social? What did it mean to Archie? His lawyer told the police they were separated, and that night Archie slept with Winona. Once. Twice. Up in the Thayer mansion on Telegraph Hill it was empty, Mrs. Archibald Thayer was at Waterman's Funeral Parlor being embalmed. Waterman's men were handling the body, which had been a virgin, never handled by anyone but Archie. Up to the night she and Archie were married, no man except her doctors had seen or touched her. At Waterman's undertaking place, they had to wipe the blood from her forehead.

At the ranch, Archie poured a glass of champagne, swallowed it. He had more money than anyone in California. If he wanted to, he could marry her. Did she want that? For a change? Married to Dennis had been nice. Would Archie want any children? He had the ones with his wife, why would he want another?

Catherine's funeral was over, and she would be buried in her family plot. "Catherine Brownlow Thayer," the stone would read. She'd be buried next to her mother.

Archie and Winona at the ranch made plans to go to Paris. A suite at the Ritz, overlooking the Ritz garden, the Place Vendome side was too noisy.

They sailed on the *Ile de France.* Could a boat be sexy? The *Ile de France* was. The passengers, the ship, the food, the sense that something was going on behind every stateroom door. And was. Dress for dinner, Winona in Madame Frances's shiny dresses. Late September, 1929, dresses were short, and for evening Madame Frances featured sequins and feathers. Archie's dinner jackets were Earl Benham, navy blue. The *Ile de France* was a broad-minded ship. The room steward unlocked the door of Winona's cabin that connected with Archie's rose-brocaded suite.

In California Catherine's will was being probated, the marble cross with "Catherine Brownlow Thayer" was being chiseled out. Up on the main deck in the Boite de Nuit, Archie and Winona were foxtrotting to Noel Coward's "Parisian Pierrot." At their table was the silver bucket of Veuve Cliquot champagne that Winona now loved. "Archie, remember the first champagne you ever had?"

He lifted his glass. "To you, I wish everybody could have a look!"

"The first champagne *I* ever had tasted sour and made me burp. I was fourteen and at the Palm Garden Restaurant. I'd talked the gentleman boarder at the Whitman's cottage at the lake into taking us to the cabaret and he ordered champagne and caviar. They both tasted horrid, but I knew it was great to say I liked it. Also, I wanted to make a hit with him, Mr. Wilson, the boarder, he lived at the Union Club, St. Paul. He was on my list of men who would keep me."

"How did Wilson connect?"

"My girlfriend Anna—it was her house we were staying—she played the piano. She'd bang out, 'Too Much Mustard' and I'd whirl around in a dance all by myself and Mr. Wilson watched. Outside too many flies. Sometimes I'd kick high so I knew he could see my drawers."

"That's all the material you thought you had to get

him to keep you? Flies outside and seeing your drawers?"

"I talked it over with my girlfriend. She thought he
liked me but would never keep me. 'He's putty in my
hands,' I told her."

"But you weren't after putty in your hands as much
as Mr. Wilson's dick."

` The captain bowed to Winona. He turned to Archie.
"May I have the next dance with this beauty?"

"You're in command of this ship, but I'm in command
of my girl, captain. How do you say it in French? . . .
Je vous en fous!"

The captain laughed and went over to a lady at the
next table.

Coming out of their cabin one night, a man was rolling
around on the floor. Delerium tremens. Archie and
Winona stepped over him. Two proper American
women stood glaring. "This would never have happened
on an *English* ship!" They watched the ship's doctor and
his assistant gather up the passed-out passenger.

The suite at the Paris Ritz could only be a suite at the
Paris Ritz. It could not have been London, or Berlin, or
New York, or Madrid. It had to be the *Paris* Ritz.

Lunch in the Ritz garden, everyone there. Noel Coward, London's new star in his play he'd written, was
wearing a pink shirt with a stiff pink collar. The Mahara-
jah of Kapurthala, an emerald in his lapel. Mr. Hiram
Bloomingdale, owner of Bloomingdale Brothers Department Store in New York. Young Woolie Donahue, son
of Mrs. Jessie Donahue, heir to F. W. Woolworth's five-

and-ten-cent stores. The Ritz garden, where you saw everybody. Archie knew a lot of the everybodies and liked how they stared at Winona.

Winona liked it, too. Archie was great. Great in bed, a great spender, he bought her twelve Lanvin dresses, and four bathing suits at Schiaparelli's. They'd be going to the Hotel du Cap at Antibes, where Madame Lanvin said all anybody needed were bathing suits and evening dresses.

Besides dresses, Archie bought her a string of pink pearls at Cartier's on the Rue de la Paix. "They match her tits," he told the Cartier salesman. It was a fact. He stopped in at Kuhn, Loeb and bought her a thousand shares of Calumet & Hecla Copper, a thousand shares of Kennicott Copper. They would be added to the brokerage account Morty had first set up for her and then further added to by Julius.

Late afternoon out to dance on the terrace of the Chateau Madrid off the Bois. There, too, were the same Maharajahs, fewer Maharanees, the Duke of Devonshire with his Duchess, all the International Set. Casino de Paris star Mistinguette with her Portuguese deposed king, who had given her the famous rope of pearls.

Back at the Ritz, Winona's Lanvin dress came off, warm early October air came through the Ritz gardenside windows. Winona wore her string of pink pearls. Did she ever look so inviting? Red curly hair cut short, red curly hair where he was, shorter and more curly.

Dinner in the Bois at Armenonville. Rich Americans, rich English, all foreigners. Daisy Fellowes with the Ali Kahn.

Archie looked at her. "She's a legend," he said. "My

cousin, young Crittenden, saw Daisy at his sister Marthe's at-home. No one saw them speak. She left. Soon after, *he* left. She and he were next heard of in their villa on the Cote d'Azur, the little town of Ramatuel. That was before she was Mrs. Fellowes. She was the Princesse de Broglie. A cable arrived. Daisy showed it to Crittenden. The old Prince de Broglie was dead. 'We separated, but for the children I must go to Paris. I'll be back here in a week.' Crittenden drove her to the station. Loving farewell, 'In a week,' a long kiss. 'In a week.' He went back to the villa, on the bedpillow was a note, 'I never want to see you again.' "

"What did he do?" asked Winona.

"He's drifting around somewhere. He never connected with people again."

Winona looked over at the former Daisy de Broglie, now become Mrs. Reggie Fellowes.

"We talked about it, but let's *go.* Everybody used to go to Cannes, but it's Antibes, they say. Hijinks at the Hotel du Cap. We'll go."

At the hotel he rang the hall porter. "Blue Train tomorrow night. Book us a suite, Hotel du Cap . . . three days, maybe four . . . we're keeping our suite here." He hung up. "Want to get married?"

"All right." All right?

Archie picked up the phone. "Hall porter . . . Archibald Thayer. I want to get married tomorrow before lunch . . . Sixteenth Arrondissement, that's where all Americans go . . . Protestant, Protestant. I'm a widower. She's divorced . . . Before lunch and tell the garden to hold a table for two at one-thirty."

77

HOTEL DU CAP full of everybody. Everybody down the
walk to Eden Roc Club—restaurant, pool, and lapping its
front wall the green blue Mediterranean, decorating it a
white steam yacht, a big one. And others.

Archie knew everyone. Everyone knew Archie. Big
party at Eden Roc for Irene Castle. On the phone, *"Veux
parler avec Madame Castle . . .* Irene, it's Archie, I want to
come to the party tonight . . . We'll be there. A big wet
kiss!" To Winona, "Everybody'll hate you because you
got 'em beat even with your clothes on. The one to look
out for is Irene. She can top anybody but not you. Know
why I know that? She's got a chilly underneath. She's
not crazy about doing it."

At nine the party began. Movie director Rex Ingram
and his movie star wife Alice Terry were giving it. From
their film studio at Nice were klieg lights planted all over
the Roc named Eden. No party could be too beautiful for
Irene Castle, grace itself, beauty and dazzle. The party
Rex and Alice had planned nearly matched Irene.

She stood on a rock, a breeze blowing softly around
her to let the party see Irene's beauty outlined in fluttery
turquoise chiffon. In the breeze it outlined the slender

line-drawing that was Irene Castle. She looked like a figurehead on the prow of the chic ship Eden Roc.

Who was taking off with Daisy Fellowes in the white white motor tender from her yacht? Why leave the party? With Daisy was her current lover, young, skinny, black shock of hair, bare from the waist up, his neck strung with Daisy's fabulous pearls, her rope of diamonds and the emerald collar. Gertie Sanford and Maurice Le Gendre were also with her. Watching from Eden Roc were sister Janie Sanford and brother Sidney Le Gendre. The four had returned from a long African safari, companionship continuing. Might Maurice marry Gertie, might Sidney marry Janie?

The tender sped along, picked up by the movie lights that shone bright on Daisy's silver sequin jacket, on her jewels on her suntanned lover. Her yacht's white-uniformed sailor at the wheel, it sparkled its course out to the horizon between navy blue sea and navy blue sky. Where? They passed her steam yacht *Soeur Blanche,* way out to the horizon? Look! Everybody did.

A gasp! On water skis, in her white satin to-the-ankle evening dress was Gertie. Beside her on water skis, Maurice, white dinner jacket, black trousers. They held the thick white ropes attached to Daisy's tender and were off. Gertie Sanford and Maurice Le G. rode the navy blue horizon like two Pegasi. Two figures by Tanagra? What things to write to Newport. To Southampton. A letter to Pride's Crossing, to write about to anywhere, because it could only happen at Eden Roc.

Archie and his new wife were welcomed into the circle. He knew Irene, he knew the Sanfords' brother Laddie, whom Winona had watched playing polo. She and

Laddie had eyed each other appreciatively. Rich, rich, rich, good-looking, a brain that functioned sparingly except on a horse, with his hand on a polo mallet. On Winona's hand was the square-cut diamond wedding ring Archie had bought two days ago at Rue de la Paix Cartier's.

Irene's party was over. Next night to Elsa Maxwell's ball at Monte Carlo to open the rubber beach. No beach for the Monegasques, so Elsa had one made and put in place. Monte Carlo was *"reconnaissant."* Grateful to American Elsa.

Sailing from Antibes to Monte Carlo aboard the black yacht of rich who-was-he? Whoever he was, the boat was a beauty, owned by the young Frenchman sent over to New York to work in a bank in some humble position at some humble salary to eke out his humble means when, would you believe, five relatives died, one, two, three, four, five, and left him sole heir to a massive fortune. Not a cousin, niece, nephew to stand in his way. He grieved not but enjoyed. He had never thought about black yachts but with all that legacy, have one.

Antibes to Monte Carlo on a summer afternoon, bathing suits brought along. Off St. Jean-Cap Ferrat, black yacht cut her engine, white rope ladder and white canvas platform were hoisted over the side. Everybody dove off, dropped off, slid off into St. Jean-Cap Ferrat's pale green water. Who was who? Elsa was already at Monte Carlo, but Prince Obolensky was on board, also a Rhode Island Pell, a Philadelphia Warburton. Winona thought about Lily Corey's Philadelphia Mr. Dahl. Everybody was beautiful, everybody went for a swim, everybody had a cabin to undress and dress in, everybody had a second bathing suit to change to and lie on the deck after. Cushions, talk, things served. As it got darker, back to the cabin to put on evening dress for the ball. Maids dried the bathing suits, packed them, and they were put in the limousines to take the guests back to Antibes after christening the rubber beach and hijinks at the ball.

Archie and Winona went back in the Rolls with Janie and black yacht's owner, who sat on the floor at Janie's feet proposing marriage, but Janie didn't know if she'd accept.

"Will you marry *me?*" Archie asked Winona. "Oh, you *did!*"

Next night they were on the Blue Train speeding across France to the Paris Ritz.

The bags were brought up, a maid was unpacking. The phone rang. "Cable."

"Joe Bickerton," the cable was signed. The bottom had fallen out of the New York Stock Exchange. Joe Bickerton was covering for Archie. Joe was reassuring . . . it was panic for a day. Archie cabled Bickerton to cover for Winona.

Another cable. The panic had doubled. Joe would save what he could. "Get back."

Archie called the Ritz porter who had received many benefices from him.

He would do what he could.

Archie crossed the Ritz porter's palm with diamonds, or the price thereof.

Everybody was doing it. Every ship was booked. How could it happen? How could everybody one day have the pull to get anything, next day nobody could get any-where? Or if they could, had they the money to pay for it?

Cables flew back and forth. In the Ritz Bar, where there was more news than in the newspapers, who should come in but Dennis Ryan. He had left the stage, joined the Jules Bache brokerage company and become a partner. He kissed Winona, shook hands with Archie.

"She used to be *my* wife, but I'm sure you only want to hear what Bache and Company think is happening and do I know how I can get you on a boat?"

Suddenly loneliness swept over Winona. How did she give up Dennis? All the things rushed back, the meeting that night in the snow, the College Inn, the red velvet dress that came off, she was in his arms, "the lessons," the wedding, then being pregnant. His child, how old would it be? All she said was, "Dennis, I knew you gave up acting and I knew you loved business, but you must be great to be a partner in Jules Bache!"

"You're too beautiful! Do you know that?" Then he kissed her again. "For other times," he said to Archie. "From New York the word is *get back.* The Cunard Line is letting down the maritime law. Wives, husbands, girl-friends, pansies can squeeze into one cabin. It's up to the passengers themselves. I'm not a pansy and I haven't got a girlfriend. I've got a wife, but she's at our house in Mount Kisco with our three kids."

"All Catholics?" asked Winona. "Remember how the priest wanted me to sign a paper before we got married and swear any children would have to be Catholics? I said I'd sign because I didn't want any and you didn't care then and then the mayor in Chicago said *he* wanted to marry us."

Dennis nodded. "But then Cathleen said she *had* to be Catholic so she could sin all she wanted to and be forgiven. She's one hell of a knockout so I got roped in again. And the kids all belong to the Pope. But *here* I've got an ex-wife, and, Archie, you've got a wife, to share an outside cabin for two on the D-deck of the *Mauretania* sailing tomorrow, boat train leaving the Gare St. Lazare at 9:00 A.M."

"Okay if I kiss you right on the mouth?" asked Archie.

"We'll make it a daisy chain. You kiss me on the mouth, I'll kiss Winona. See you 9:00 A.M. Gare St. Lazare, I'll have the tickets."

78

THE *MAURETANIA* crossing was different from the trip over on the *Ile de France.* Very. Everyone panicking, everyone waiting for a wireless or sending one. The weather was perverse. Serene skies in October? The ship steady as the Staten Island ferry, Indian-summer warmth, everything calm except the passengers.

Joe Bickerton stuck to his client. "HAD TO SELL NOB HILL HOLDING."

"STILL COVERING. STILL HOLDING THE RANCH."

"CANNOT HOLD."

Archie went up on the boat deck. A clear, unruffled night. What was left? He had never earned a cent. Had never had the need to or the wish. A ten-goal man in the Marin Polo Club, what could that earn him? He could be a polo coach, but who had a polo team left? He was handsome. He was a guy who knew how to enjoy and how to make someone else enjoy, but after that? Zero. Where could he go? What could he do? The legacy had gone. The vast California lands he was left from his grandfather, more from his mother and father, had to be sold. The choice narrowed down.

He went over the rail.

A loud splash nobody heard.

The ship was making twenty-four knots and did not stop to count her passengers.

79

ALONE.

She'd never been alone. Glorieta, Winona, Chicago, New York, Palm Beach, San Francisco, Paris, Antibes. In thirty years she'd been with someone. Now she was in New York alone.

With Dennis the first time, then Morty. And so on and

so on. When did Dennis and she get here? Looking back, it seemed like the only memories were "on and on and on," like what the first year Latin teacher used to say to the class at Winona High School . . . *"ad infinitum."*

Nothing had changed in the stock market. People's stuff was gone and stayed gone.

Now what? Go back into a show? Flo's Follies was on tour and no more Frolic on the New Amsterdam Roof.

Joe Bickerton had met the boat. Took her to the Algonquin. He said there was a chance to hang onto some of her stock, to let him have anything cashable. She handed him her jewel case. He'd sell and try to cover. The bellboy showed her to a single bedroom on the court that she had told Mr. Mitchell, clerk at the desk, "would be temporary."

Mr. Mitchell read the unspoken language of *in the chips* or *broke.* A language desk clerks are all fluent in.

She rang up the Ziegfeld office. "It's Winona Lloyd."

"Oh, hello," said the girl on the switchboard.

"Is Mr. Ziegfeld in?"

"No, he hasn't come in today."

"Let me speak to Goldie."

Goldie was Mr. Ziegfeld's secretary for how many years. "Hello, Winona, I heard you got married and were in Paris."

"Goldie, I have to talk to him. Say to call me, I'm at the Algonquin, suite ten-oh-two." Why say room when suite has only one letter more?

The phone rang. "It's Goldie. I didn't get him, but I got Sidney. He knows more about where he is and where he *will* be than the governor. Sidney says he'll have luncheon at the Knickerbocker Grill with Harry Sinclair and be here in the office at three. If you're around, drop up. I'll tell him you might."

"Thanks, Goldie, I'll be there."

Her luggage filled up the small room. Hard to do with no space, but she got the wardrobe trunk open. Archie had bought it for her at the shop on the Champs-Elysées a nice old gentleman owned. His name was Monsieur Vuitton and he said they made all their trunks to order. It cost two hundred dollars in American money. He wrote the number of it in a book. She took out a Lanvin red suit, just right for early November. It had a squirrel collar, squirrel cuffs. She'd thought of Captain Humphrey's Nutty when she'd ordered the suit, but she didn't think of Nutty today or Captain Humphrey or anybody. Today she thought the squirrel fur made her look young, soft-looking. She'd never gotten to look hard. The looking glass bolstered up her courage. Gray fur against her neck, the suit the color of holly berries. What did she have to worry about?

"He's in and not on the telephone, go ahead." Goldie pointed the way, though she didn't need to.

He was at his big French carved walnut with gold inlay desk.

"Flo."

"Hello, dear, you look lovely."

Did they kiss?

They did as if they didn't.

"Still got your great shape. Sit down. Did you get hit like the rest of us?"

"I thought I had my jewelry left, but what I didn't take with me I left in the safe deposit box with my stocks and when everything was sliding Joe Bickerton sold it trying to cover."

" 'Trying to cover,' is the theme song today."

"Flo, I want to go back to work."

"Yes, dear. My God, you have beautiful legs. You and Marilyn have the most beautiful legs of anybody in all my shows. When you pulled the blue velvet curtain across the stage with your bottom and one leg bare! Have you still got the freckles? I used to wish people could see it out front. I wish I had something, dear, but I don't. The Follies is playing Chicago, but you wouldn't want to tour and anyway they're all full up. Try George White. He has his Scandals on."

"I won't be foxy, Flo. I need something now."

"Sweetie, how old are you?"

"Only thirty."

"You were . . . what were you?"

"Twenty-two when you left for Marilyn."

"I read you were married to Archibald Thayer. They said he was one of the richest men in California."

"It's gone. And Archie."

"It was in the papers. A lot of people took the short-cut. You knew a lot of people. Morty, of course, is married. Damn pretty girl, gave him a baby." . . .

Winona went back to the Algonquin. George White? The Scandals? All right. His secretary said he would see her. Maybe the same red, squirrel-trimmed suit? Maybe try another, she hadn't made it with that. A rose-colored coat with mink sleeves and collar. From Lanvin. A beauty.

It was distracting, Flo not having anything, not even interest. Fill up the time, get doing something. Something that didn't cost much. She walked to the corner of Fifth Avenue, took the bus going up to Riverside Drive. At Eighty-second Street she got off, there was her house, a nurse with a fine dark-blue baby carriage going in the door.

Georgie White sat behind his desk looking like her mother's old description of New York men. White-faced, dark hair slicked back, shiny like patent leather, white silk shirt and it wasn't even Sunday. He and Ann Pennington were the stars of the Scandals. He was a great dancer, she was adorable, looked like a little girl with dimpled knees and a long pigtail, and sexy.

"Nothing doing now, and the next Scandals I don't know if I'll raise the money. I always had a yen for you, you still look great." He laughed a sardonic laugh. "Y'know what they say, 'You're young, you're *not* young, you're looking *great.*'" He laughed again. "Know what you could still do? Smoke out a rich fella. Don't let them tell you there aren't any. Get one and give up show business. You got *IT* to offer for private entertainment. For the footlights, y'gotta be in your teens, early twenties."

Back at the Algonquin.
Where was Peggy Hopkins? She rang up Goldie and got Peggy's number.
Peggy was away in Texas. Mr. and Mrs. Joyce were at their ranch.
Archie had loved his ranch. Joe said that was the last to go.
Try Julius? Mr. Schwab's secretary took the message.

Julius did not return the call.

One minute free and easy, everything she wanted. Next minute, disaster, death, more disaster, then one blank after another. Zero.

Eva Dill was in a play at the Cort Theatre. Not the lead, but a featured part. Had Eva forgiven her for Rex? Probably not, though now she was divorced from him. Rex? His name was in the theatre ads, he was in *Say When,* at the Shubert Theatre co-starred with London's Emmy Wehlen. Rex? Should she? She phoned Goldie. Did they have Rex Cherry's number? No, but try the Lambs Club, he'd be a member.

"Rex Cherry?" she asked the Lambs' operator.

"Just a minute."

"Hello?"

"Rex?"

"Yes."

"Rex, this is Winona Lloyd."

"Who?"

"Winona. Remember Mrs. Newbury's in Chicago? And the Virginia Hotel?"

"Is it still red?"

"Want to find out?"

"I thought you got married to the richest man in California."

"I did, but it's over. I'm here temporarily at the Algonquin."

"I'm at the Shubert. Want to meet after the show?"

"Where?"

"I live out on Long Island in Great Neck, but I keep a place at the Astor. Say, eleven-thirty? Number three-oh-one. I'll tell them at the desk you'll be up."

"Three-oh-one."

"Bring the red stuff."

She laughed and rang off.

Around the corner on Sixth Avenue was the Rotisserie, where sometimes she and Dennis had gone. It was great. And cheap, and hadn't changed. Dennis always ordered dark meat, she had white.

Back at the hotel, Mr. Mitchell handed her the key and a message.

> Sorry about tonight. My wife is coming in.
> Will call you.
>
> Rex.

80

ANYTHING IN *The Passing Show?* The Shuberts were always doing musicals. *The Passing Show* wasn't classy like the Follies, but was where Flo had stolen Marilyn from to be in his Follies.

Mr. J. J. Shubert would see her. His apartment was on the top floor of the office building opposite the Shubert Theatre. He and his brother Lee owned the office building as well as the Shubert Theatre. Ma Simmons, the Shubert pansy casting director, saw her. Of course remembered her. Wasn't sure if there was anything. Mr. J. J. looked in, looked her over, knew he was looking at Ziegfeld's old girl. Didn't *look* old. Maybe do for him? If Ziegfeld didn't go for her, should he? He gave the signal to Ma.

"We'll see," said Ma, and walked with her to the door. "You're where we can reach you?"

"The Algonquin."

"Of course."

Walking along Forty-fourth Street to the hotel, who was that walking beside her?

"Hello."

"Hello." It was Eddie Schmidt, Ziegfeld's bookkeeper, who used to give Winona her salary envelope, and Ellie would bawl him out because he'd come in without knocking and if she had nothing on he'd fumble around with his pay envelopes while he got a good stare. Ellie threatened to bat him, but he said, "I'm doing my job, you do yours and if you don't want me to see her ass, get her into some clothes."

He was walking along beside her. "A fortune-teller told me I'd meet a redhead if I walked east. Buy you a drink?"

They were in front of the Penwick. He knocked on the door, someone looked out.

"Eddie Schmidt."

The door opened. He was shown to a table.

"What will it be? You like a Bronx?"

"What is it?"

"Orange juice and gin."

"All right."

The waiter went away.

"What are y'doing?"

"I just got home from abroad."

"I read about it. Your hubby died."

The two Bronx cocktails came. Eddie paid. He raised his glass. "To the next."

"What does that mean?"

"The guy lucky enough to get you."

She looked at him. Was he awful? He looked all right, did he have any money? He was one of the ones that did. He didn't live on his fortune, he lived on his salary. Maybe? Till something happened? Till she could think of something? Or someone? Or what? "Any offers?"

"Y'mean y'might try me out? It's Ninety-sixth and Broadway."

Winona nodded. "Two more," he hollered at the waiter. "Make 'em stronger."

The waiter set them down. Eddie paid. Held up his glass. "To you know what!"

They drank.

"The El gets us there quick, get an express. Y'mean I can really look at you without Ellie barking at me?"

The two Bronxes had hit Winona. "To Ninety-sixth and Broadway! The place!"

81

July, 1930. Winona lay on Eddie's sagging bed. What had gone wrong? The Crash had knocked everything and everybody sideways, had knocked her on her canetta, nobody available, no money. Only Eddie. Eddie had a job, a savings account. Now she was thirty-one, was that the end? How old was Mrs. Brigham when she and rich Mr. Penniman married? Thirty-one was only old in the Follies, Scandals, *Passing Shows*. She told Flo she was thirty. George White thought she should give up, but why? Why couldn't she get back in the swing? Not the Ziegfeld Frolic Swing, but why give up? She'd let herself go, but a little money could fix her up. She went back to *The Daily Mirror,* poured some coffee, turned to Winchell. What was that about Minnesota?

> James Sefton Holbrook, recently elected president of the Minnesota Chemical Corporation, International, the powerhouse of the Midwest, newly divorced, was making eyes at the wife of Chaney Riddle, president of Canadian Aluminium that owns the financial

half of Toronto. The lady seems willing to collect presidents.

Where was he staying? Winchell didn't give that away. What if she tried the Ambassador Hotel? The Ritz, where she and Flo had got started after the Crystal Ballroom's Sixty Club John Paul Jones dance? The Waldorf? James Sefton Holbrook. James Sefton Holbrook. *Sure . . .* Mr. Holbrook's boy that played ball in the backyard of their house on Wabasha. What if she got cuted up? In the kitchen drawer was the rent. See what it could get? Across Broadway was the pink sign "Chez LuLu" with beauty parlor pictures. In the window, a long blonde wig. The rent money would take care of a henna rinse, a dress, shoes, bra.

Chez LuLu's toned up her natural color. Shady Lady, down Broadway, displayed some useful dresses. On a model a yellow chiffon nightgown showed everything if a model had had anything to show. She chose it and a black dress, sexy, not tarty. Black suede shoes. A pink satin bra with ideas. Winona laughed when she looked in the glass. She looked like a lady who could but didn't feature it. Call the Ambassador Hotel.

"Mr. James Sefton Holbrook."

"Not registered."

The Ritz. Not there.

The Waldorf Towers. "Who's calling Mr. Holbrook?"

"Winona Lloyd."

"Winona Lloyd?"

"Winona Lloyd."

"His line is engaged."

"I'll hold on."

Winona's thoughts went back to Wabasha Street, the Holbrook boys tossing ball in their backyard, her in the hammock on the upstairs porch of the Sanburn Street house, watching them, thinking of their father.

"I can ring through now."

"This is Mr. Holbrook's secretary."

"This is Winona Lloyd."

A pause, then another man's voice, not old, not young, authoritative, juicy, direct, important, no time to waste. *"Who* is this?"

"Winona Lloyd. Remember me from Sanburn Street? *You* lived on Wabasha. I used to watch you and your brother play ball."

"My God!" He laughed. Winona laughed. "Winona?"

"Jim?"

"Where are you?"

"About ten blocks away."

"I'm getting dressed to go to dinner. Want to come by for a drink?"

"Sure."

"Twenty-four C, the Towers entrance on Fiftieth Street. I'll tell the desk you're expected."

"Jim?"

"Yuh?"

"Did you think this would happen when you woke up this morning?"

He laughed. "Still got red hair?"

"All the places." She laughed and rang off.

82

"TWENTY-FOUR C. Mr. Holbrook."

"He's expecting you."

A glance in the lobby mirror. Good lighting. Chez LuLu had given her hair a great shine. The elevator purred up to the twenty-fourth. The sign in the hall said "A to H TURN RIGHT." There it was, 24C. Last night Eddie, tonight 24C?

Twenty-four C door opened.

"Jim."

He laughed. "My God! You're the little girl that grew into a knockout." He closed the door. "I don't believe I'm looking at you."

"At *some* of me."

She leaned forward. Her lips rested on his. Hers were soft and wet. His were hard. Were they rough? The hard lips knew what to do. "Remember when I lifted you up to ride piggyback with your legs around my neck?"

"Want to try it now?" She laughed and the hard mouth covered hers. Again.

"You had the softest-haired pussy I ever felt."

"And never saw. But your father did. He was my first."

"I don't blame the old sonofabitch. Am I going to see it?"

"But what about, 'Want to come over for a drink? I have to go out to dinner.'" She laughed and the Shady Lady black dress was on the floor, nothing under it but the pink satin bra with ideas. "This comes off." She looked through the door to his bedroom. "Is that a bed?" This time last night Eddie had had a beer too many and needed help. Tonight the same legs stretched wide and Jim Holbrook was as horny as his father and had the equipment.

"Oh my God! Oh my God!" He lay back. "How many years since that backyard?" He put his hand up the inside of her leg, felt where his father's rough thumb made her know about that place. "You feel great. Come back to Minnie with me? We'll pay off whoever you're with."

"You won't need to."

"I want somebody I can grab whenever. In-between board meetings if I feel like it. Somebody that loves it. I was married to Alice Power up on Prospect and we have four boys, all grown-up. But Alice hated when the business started skyrocketing and Minnie Chemicals International Limited put me in a bunch that didn't take to Alice. She got dowdy and fat and liked comfort and only put up with fucking. I asked her if she wanted a divorce. She asked the boys and they said if she wanted to, so she has a big farm over at Rollingstone and the settlement is two million dollars." He put his hand on her. His thumb was smooth.

"Alice couldn't wait for it to be over, but *you* keep asking for it. I wish it was just for me, but I know experience when I'm inside it. I had a plain, dutiful wife, now I'd like Mrs. James Sefton Holbrook to keep wanting one more."

He went out to another room, his secretary was taking a call. "Ring off." He didn't bother to close the door.

Winona lay on the king-size bed.

"Talk to whoever you'll need, I'm getting married, Harry, as soon as you get it set up. I'm unattached and so is Mrs. Winona Lloyd Thayer. Widow since how long?" He shouted back to the king-size bed.

"Nineteen twenty-nine, October."

She got up and stood in the doorway, yellow chiffon from Shady Lady concealing nothing. Harry Edwards fastened his eyes on the desk.

Jim laughed. "Meet the new Mrs. Holbrook, Harry. Did you ever get one like that? Get the date set up tomorrow, I've got a board meeting Thursday when I'm due back."

They returned to the bedroom. This time he closed the door. "Win darling, I've got my own private car. Mrs. James Sefton Holbrook will *know* she's Mrs. James Sefton Holbrook when she leaves my Pullman palace's big soft bed and gets out at the Minnie station." His hand went under the Shady Lady yellow chiffon nightgown. "You're beautiful."

"And I'm thirty-one."

He laughed and gathered her close to him.